WITH
UN
WINCHESTER
D1615065
KA 0425460 0

CRITICAL REFLECTIONS ON HUMAN RIGHTS AND THE ENVIRONMENT

Series Editors: Anna Grear, *Cardiff Law School, UK, University of Waikato, New Zealand and Global Network for the Study of Human Rights and the Environment (GNHRE)*, Karen Morrow, *University of Swansea, Wales, UK* and Evadne Grant, *University of the West of England, UK*

This book series investigates themes at the intersection of human rights and the environment, bringing key issues and challenges to the centre of contemporary debate and reflection. The series presents imaginative, critically engaging reflections that aim to reconfigure our understanding of questions inhabiting the relationship between human rights and the environment and human beings and the living world in an age of multiple crises. Critical Reflections on Human Rights and the Environment is a forum for provocative, 'beyond the boundaries' thinking. The Series Editors welcome proposals from imaginative scholars with a passion for understanding, transformation and the building of alternative future histories.

Critical Reflections on Ownership

Mary Warnock

Oxford University, UK

CRITICAL REFLECTIONS ON HUMAN RIGHTS AND THE ENVIRONMENT

Cheltenham, UK • Northampton, MA, USA

Published by
Edward Elgar Publishing Limited
The Lypiatts
15 Lansdown Road
Cheltenham
Glos GL50 2JA
UK

Edward Elgar Publishing, Inc.
William Pratt House
9 Dewey Court
Northampton
Massachusetts 01060
USA

A catalogue record for this book
is available from the British Library

Library of Congress Control Number: 2015933446

This book is available electronically in the **Elgar**online
Law subject collection
DOI 10.4337/9781781955482

ISBN 978 1 78195 546 8 (cased)
ISBN 978 1 78195 547 5 (paperback)
ISBN 978 1 78195 548 2 (eBook)

Typeset by Servis Filmsetting Ltd, Stockport, Cheshire
Printed and bound in Great Britain by T.J. International Ltd, Padstow

Contents

Editorial introduction

Anna Grear, Karen Morrow and Evadne Grant

In the context of critical reflections upon the relationship between human rights and the environment, it is difficult to imagine many themes more central to the human–environmental nexus than that of 'ownership'. Lying at the heart of the widely impugned subject–object relations that set up the human as 'master' (and 'owner') of the earth and its living order, the notion of ownership raises a profoundly natural–cultural (in the rich sense evoked by Haraway[1]) knot of puzzles and dilemmas. The impulse towards forms of what we can broadly think of as 'ownership' is, at one level, deeply 'natural'. Such impulses can be read, for example, in the struggle within and between various non-human animal species for territory, burrows, warmth and food.

Humans have, of course, turned 'ownership' impulses into something more complex and institutionalised. The human institution of ownership has long formed a contested theme in political and legal theory, and 'ownership' has often featured in fraught questions of intra- and inter-species justice. Some humans have even deployed notions of 'ownership' (and closely related justifications drawing upon a 'natural' entitlement to 'property') as a legitimation for historical and contemporary practices of dispossession. Salient examples include the extensive enclosure of the commons in the service of industrial agriculture in England;[2] the dispossession of indigenous peoples under European colonialism;[3] predatory neo-colonialisms

[1] D. Haraway, *When Species Meet* (University of Minnesota Press, Minneapolis MN 2007).

[2] See, for example, E.M. Wood, *The Origins of Capitalism* (The Monthly Press, New York 1999) at 67–94.

[3] J. McLean, 'The transnational corporation in history: lessons for today?' (2004) 79 *Indiana Law Journal* 363–77.

imposed on the global South;[4] global industrial ravaging of the environmental commons;[5] asymmetrically distributed patterns of privilege and privation even *within* the global North;[6] and the internal predatory extension of neo-colonial practices embraced by elites in the global South at the expense of the poor in general and indigenous peoples in particular.[7]

It is perhaps no accident that historically patterned, familiar injustices congealing around legitimations based upon an appeal to 'ownership', 'mastery' and entitlement have tended to reflect the fact that socioeconomic dominance – and the related enjoyment of 'ownership' – has most often been the possession of the 'master subject' of Western political, economic and legal theory: the white, European, property-owner–citizen *homo politicus–economicus–juridicus*. Certainly, historically (and contemporaneously in many cultures by effectively replicating and propagating all aspects of the Western master subject paradigm bar its 'whiteness', effectively extending its reach to newly constituted male political, economic and legal elites) this has been a recognised and relatively stubborn pattern. In either case, women, children, the nomadic, the indigenous and/or other marginalised human groups have not been/are not quintessential exercisers of 'ownership' rights. This particular construct of the 'owner'

---

4 See, for just one example of an extensive literature on specific cases of corporate malpractice and state complicity, C. Kamphuis, 'Foreign mining, law and the privatization of property: a case study from Peru' (2012) 3/2 *Journal of Human Rights and the Environment* 217–53. More generally, see, for example, C. Jochnick, 'Confronting the impunity of non-state actors: new fields for the promotion of human rights' (1999) 21 *Human Rights Quarterly* 21, 56–79 at 65; S. Joseph, 'Taming the Leviathans: multinational enterprises and human rights' (1999) *46 Netherlands International Law Review* 171, 173–4; and the reports of the Special Rapporteur to the Commission on Human Rights on the dumping of toxic waste: Commission on Human Rights (20 January 1998).

5 See, for example, L. Westra, 'Environmental rights and human rights: the final Enclosure Movement', in R. Brownsword (ed.), *Global Governance and the Quest for Justice: Volume 4: Human Rights* (Hart, Oxford 2004) 107–19.

6 Increasingly apparent under the pressures of recent austerity doctrine.

7 See, for example, discussion in E. Burke III and K. Pomeranz (eds), *The Environment in World History* (University of California Press, Berkeley CA 2009).

has particular implications for the human–environmental nexus. The ontology of modern 'man', as is well known, builds upon a problematic subject–object split fully reflected in 'man's' position as the agential and epistemic 'centre' of the world[8] – a position of assumed mastery thoroughly associated with long patterns of environmental degradation and well-rehearsed practices of human intra-species injustice.

Ownership then, is a subject of pivotal importance to critical reflections on the multifaceted and complex relationship between human rights and the environment.

Warnock offers an extended engagement with this important theme. The brief of the *Critical Reflections* series for authors is to offer a relatively unconstrained critical reflection upon a theme relevant to the nexus of human rights and the environment. Warnock begins by asking a threshold philosophical question: 'can absolutely anything be owned?' and subsequently refines her discussion by carefully confining the scope of her inquiry to the ownership of 'property' (itself a subject of immense importance for the theme of this book series). Her writing is an enriching mix of the personal, the autobiographical, the philosophical, the political and the legal brought into lyrical engagement with the questions of what ownership means and what difference ownership makes.

Warnock's reflective journey takes her readers from an account of the origins of society and property as a social institution, into the intimate realms of ownership in action in an almost phenomenological meditation upon 'gardening', characterised by contemplating the relationships between property, intimacy and privacy. Here, Warnock is at her most self-revealing – almost autobiographical in tone and focus – carefully foregrounding her discussion in a personal meditation on the power of affective and aesthetic ties to a sense of place. Next, Warnock subjects broader societal notions of common ownership to a critical reflection, examining first communism and then some 'more modest forms' of common ownership, before moving on to explore the expansive vistas of the 'unowned' in the romantic idea of 'wilderness'.

It is only after offering this panoramic beginning that Warnock

---

[8] See, for example, C. Merchant, *The Death of Nature: Women, Ecology and the Scientific Revolution* (Harper Collins, New York 1980); V. Plumwood, *Feminism and the Mastery of Nature* (Routledge, London 1993).

turns her attention to the ethical implications of ownership: how do we take responsibility for the planet? The planet, for Warnock, is an 'orphan' thing – a term she uses to emphasise the impossibility of exercising ownership over 'the planet itself'. In her discussion of 'taking responsibility for the planet', Warnock calls, yet again, on the profound sense of connection to, and love for, the 'thing itself' that characterises the intimate heart of our richest human experiences of ownership – and extends it to embrace the planet – acknowledging a kind of 'love' increasingly recognised towards the environment itself and fortified by understanding the complexity and intricacy of the balance of earth-systems and the interdependencies between layers and forms of life on earth. Warnock, in a sense, opens up her autobiographically intimate journey through ownership to create a sense of a shared biographical location for human beings and to build thereon a conception of intimate responsibility towards the planet as inherent in our shared human situation – but there is more. We have arrived, Warnock insists, at a changed view of what it even means to be human – at an emphatic rejection of Cartesian dualism (and, thus, the subject–object relations of mastery). There is, she suggests, a deepening philosophical sense of our human interdependency, co-situation and kinship with multiple non-human others. This sense, she suggests, could be the beginning of a movement towards an adequate sense of responsibility for the planet. How then, she asks, can this new sense of responsibility be forged and expressed *without* recourse to empty metaphors of stewardship or by appeals to the invention of new gods (such as Gaia)?

Warnock's working position adopts a 'generally favourable view of ownership' as a form of living connection with something which is expressed in practical terms in a series of 'useful compromises'. As prosaic, in a sense, as gardening itself, ownership responsibility can express a kind of love – a kind of care – for a thing itself, and the 'useful compromises' that Warnock has in mind are instances of balancing rights of ownership with forms of access rights and other interventions that diversify the relations that communities can have with land in particular: The Countryside and Rights of Way Act 2000; the National Trust; the designation of green-belt land – all examples, as it were, of 'compromise conservation' that are as deeply British, in a way, as Warnock's passion for gardens and gardening. *Owning*, then, just as much as 'belonging', shapes our experience and ethics, generating in turn the feelings and values that are so fertile for the production of responsibility taking. But love of home alone cannot take us all the way. Research and education, in Warnock's view, become the lynchpins of future progress: they will 'lead us slowly in the direction of the goal: that we assume common responsibility for a world that we do not own, which lies beyond our backyard but which we jointly inhabit; and I also believe nothing else will do so' (see Chapter 8).

Having established why we might take responsibility for what we do own, and how that could be extended to what we do not own, Warnock confronts the final philosophical question in her critical reflection on ownership: 'why do we want to preserve the natural world?'. Here, she suggests, the answer is not love, but fear: 'Promethean fear' – a rational fear of what we ourselves have unleashed: 'fear seems to me to be a powerful motive to bring us to adapt our behaviour and even to make sacrifices of some of the things that technology has brought us. If this means that we must educate people to be afraid, then we should reflect that this is, after all, a not uncommon purpose of education' (see Chapter 9).

Warnock calls us – in the final analysis – to abandon human arrogance, calling on a sense of humility and on fear to regulate our relations with the environment. Such a call, unsurprisingly, tends to echo critical philosophical accounts challenging the human master–subject and insisting that all relations with the living order are but provisional 'cuts' made in a world newly understood, by some philosophers and scientists at least, as a space in which humans are no longer the 'centre' but thrown into the 'middle'.[9]

Warnock's rich, philosophically authoritative and refreshingly intimate reflection provides a lyrical and insightful path towards potentially transformed understandings of just 'who we are'[10] in 'the world' we share and inhabit. Warnock skilfully weaves an account of ownership that moves it away from ill-considered assumptions

---

[9] See A. Philippopoulos-Mihalopoulos (ed.), *Law and Ecology: New Environmental Foundations* (Routledge, Abingdon 2011), especially his own chapter in that collection.

[10] A persistent question underlying the epistemological enquiry in L. Code, *Ecological Thinking: The Politics of Epistemic Location* (Oxford University Press, Oxford 2006).

of exploitative human mastery towards a sensitive, nurturing, eco-engaged mode of responsibility building on something approaching a scientifically informed awe responsive to the complexities – and to the dangers – of a planetary system tipped into crisis by human historical arrogance and instrumentalism.

1. The scope of the investigation: can absolutely anything be owned?

'Well! Some people talk of morality, and some of religion, but give me a little snug property'.[1] I have in my day talked of both morality and religion, but now it is time to talk of property. Everything that is a property must have an owner, though ownership may be of things other than property, such as rights. However, in my investigation of the concept, I shall confine myself to the ownership of property, which is what 'ownership' in the commonest sense implies. For I want to discover, if I can, what it is actually like to own things, that is, what difference it makes to us whether we own something or not. But of course 'us' includes 'me'; and I am conscious that my investigation is necessarily conducted from my own point of view, and laden with my own prejudices. Properly scientific readers may therefore find it lacking in objectivity, indeed often lapsing into undisguised autobiography. I can apologise to them for this weakness but not, I fear, change its character.

I shall consider whether the private ownership of property can be judged an intrinsically good thing, or, on the contrary, whether having everything in common with other people is an ideal to which we should aspire, and whether common or shared ownership can have the same 'feel' about it as private ownership. And, crucially, I shall consider what is entailed by a thing having no owner, 'orphan' things, such as is the planet itself.

Lawyers have found it difficult to arrive at a definition of ownership. Ownership, they insist, is 'of things'. But since any possible object of discourse, from a pig to a philosophy of life, from a horse to a horoscope may be referred to as a 'thing', this does not help very much. In old-fashioned legal terminology, 'things' were called

1 Maria Edgeworth, *The Absentee* (1812) ch. 2.

'choses', and were divided into two kinds, 'choses in possession', which are material objects such as buildings or jewellery, and 'choses in action' which are rights that can be enforced by legal action. In this chapter, I shall raise the question whether absolutely any 'thing' can be owned; and without giving a definitive answer to that question, I shall at least delimit the kind of 'things' ownership of which I shall be exploring, and rule out certain others, as outside the scope of this enquiry, which will be concerned, for the most part, with 'choses in possession'.

Whatever the difficulties of defining ownership, what is certain is that ownership is a complicated relationship between people, in that, if you claim to own something, you as owner are claiming rights which other people must respect. Now to talk of rights is at once to talk in legal, or quasi-legal terms. I am perfectly aware that philosophers and politicians talk of 'natural', or 'inalienable' rights, and though we now have the Human Rights Act on the Statute Book, there is no definitive list of such rights, nor any intelligible answer to the question how they came into being. For in normal language, if I claim a right, I am implying that this right has been conferred on me either by law or in virtue of some conventional relationship, such as being your pupil, your client, your customer or your spouse. To appeal to natural or human rights thus seems to me to be to use a metaphor, though one that is easily intelligible; it supposes a natural or moral law that lies behind, or is superior to, positive law. Thus Sophocles makes Antigone declare to the tyrant Creon that she is entitled by a greater law than his to throw dust on the body of her brother. In modern parlance, she is claiming that it is a human right that people should not be prevented from burying their dead according to their own conventions of decency. Broadly speaking, then, the idea of a human right is used to define what should be the proper relationship between an individual and the state of which he is a member. Ownership confers rights, because there are ways of acquiring things that are recognised by law, or at least by convention (I shall return to this in the next chapter), and it would be a violation of those rights if the owner were to be deprived, whether by another person or by the state itself, of the enjoyment of what is his.

Ownership, it should be observed, is not the only thing that confers rights: I may have a right of way or other right of access to land created by legally recognised usage that is undoubtedly yours, not mine. But this particular right must derive from some local byelaw, to which I can appeal if you accuse me of trespass. A jealous wife may claim that she has a right to know where her husband has been passing his time, because (probably unwisely) she regards the relation between husband and wife as necessarily entailing total openness. In a civilised society, that is, one where the rule of law is established, the law will protect not only a person, but his property; thus the concept of ownership and that of law are closely linked, indeed are central to such a society. If, without my consent, you take something that is owned by me you have committed theft, a criminal offence in any society that we would consider civilised; and if there were no such thing as ownership, there would be no such offence as theft. Historically, we may assume that laws have developed largely in order to define the rights of ownership as distinct from mere possession, that is, what you actually have about your person. As A.M. Honoré put it 'A people to whom ownership was unknown, or who accorded it a minor place in their arrangements, who meant by *meum* and *tuum* no more than "what I (or you) presently hold" would live in a world that was not our world'.[2] And he later says 'When children understand that Christmas presents go not to the finder but to the child whose name is written on the outside of the parcel . . . we know they have at least an embryonic idea of ownership'.[3] It is this idea that I want to explore.

But, at the outset, we should recognise that '*meum*' and '*tuum*', 'his', 'our', 'their', though they are known in the grammar books as possessive pronouns (and sometimes referred to in America as 'ownership pronouns'), are not by any means always used to indicate ownership or possession. We speak naturally and intelligibly of 'my mother', 'my psychiatrist', 'my children' without in the least implying ownership. There is indeed a number of different uses of the possessive pronoun which absolutely cannot denote ownership. Take, for example, 'my country': while it is perfectly proper to refer to the ownership of pieces of land by the use of the possessive pronoun, as in 'my garden' or 'your field', to refer to 'my country' has no such connotation. Yet it may be used rhetorically as if it had. When the Countryside Bill was going through parliament in the year 2000, supporters of the Bill held up banners declaring 'The country

---

2 A.M. Honoré, 'Ownership', ch. 5 in A.G. Guest (ed.), *Oxford Essays in Jurisprudence* (Oxford University Press, Oxford 1961) p. 107.

3 Ibid., pp. 114–15.

is yours' and 'Give us back our country'. These slogans involved not only two senses of 'country', but two senses of 'your'. To demand the 'right to roam' is a rhetorical device aiming to suggest that 'property is theft', and yet at the same time that the countryside is owned by the ramblers.

Let us return to the legal insistence that ownership is of things. This, as we have already seen, is hopelessly inclusive. But at least the proposition was put to powerful use in the Act of Parliament of 1833, which prohibited the ownership of living persons as property, the Act which abolished slavery. 'Things' do not and may not lawfully include people. In the same year, across the Atlantic, William Lloyd Garrison formed the American Anti-Slavery Society, and in 1854 he wrote:

> I am a believer in that portion of the American Declaration of Independence in which it is set forth, as among self-evident truths, 'that all men are created equal; that they are endowed by their creator with certain inalienable rights; that among these are life, liberty and the pursuit of happiness'. Hence, I am an abolitionist. Hence I cannot but regard oppression in every form – and, most of all, that which turns a man into a thing – with indignation and abhorrence.[4]

A fellow human being is not a thing. But things may be living or inanimate; it is only human beings who are not things. I may properly enjoy full ownership of my pets.

Increasingly, moreover, 'things' that can be owned include non-physical objects, such as patents, copyright, bright ideas and the research results that are the outcome of such ideas, 'intellectual' as well as material property. Ownership of property entails, among other things, the exclusive right to the use of the property by the owner, its sale if he wishes to sell, and, as we have seen, the possibility of the charge of theft (or in the case of copyright, plagiarism or piracy) against someone who unlawfully gains access to it. All these are 'choses in action'.

It is easy to see how the concept of intellectual property arose, by analogy with material property such as land, building or jewellery. Patenting was introduced in Britain three or more centuries ago, and the law governing intellectual property has grown more and more complex and controversial since the Copyright Act of 1956.

---

[4] W.L. Garrison (1854), *The Liberator*, 4 July.

Many people still think of the world of ideas as a world within which everything should be freely shared, especially since, if I share my idea with you, or with the world at large, I am not myself deprived of it, or its use. Moreover it seems (or seemed to the Coalition government in legislation proposed in 2012, but, at the time of writing yet to be enacted) that authors and composers have a duty to help to educate the young by allowing schools and colleges free access to their works. But authors and composers as well as inventors have to live, and it would be impossible for them to do so, if the concept of intellectual property were to be abolished. More worryingly still, freedom of information legislation threatens to allow open access to research in progress at university laboratories to anyone seeking it, regardless of the danger that incomplete or misleading results might thus be published. It is to be hoped that this legislation, also proposed in 2012, will be appropriately limited.

One way or another, with the growth of information technology, as well as the insistence on transparency in public life, the enforcement of laws designed to protect the ownership of intellectual property becomes increasingly difficult, some would say impossible. At any rate in what follows, I shall not be pursuing the issues that arise in connection with intellectual property rights. I am concerned solely with the ownership of material objects. This is the primary sense of 'ownership', going along with the primary sense of 'property', and it is this primary sense that I shall attempt to investigate further in the next few chapters.

Within this class of ownership, however, there are two particular cases which give rise to controversial questions, about which I must say something here. The first is the question whether we can be said to have ownership of our own bodies, while we are alive. A body is, after all, a physical or material object, though of an exceedingly complex kind. We have seen that we may not have ownership of other people's bodies while they are alive. Such ownership is slavery, officially abolished in the mid-nineteenth century. Slavery turned a man into a thing, and in doing so deprived him of freedom to make his own decisions and choices. Those who are not slaves retain these attributes: they can each say 'I am my own person'. But we have seen that the use of the possessive pronoun does not necessarily entail ownership; and there seems something irredeemably odd about saying that I own my body, though it is undeniably mine, not yours. The oddity lies, I believe, in the fact that I am too closely connected to my body for it to be my property. I am my body: there is no 'I' separate from 'it'.

If I were René Descartes, or any other philosophical dualist, I might not find the concept of ownership of my body so strange. For Descartes famously believed that the only thing whose existence he could not doubt was the existence of himself as a thinking or doubting entity, a *res cogitans* as opposed to a *res extensa*, or physical object occupying space. 'I think, therefore I am.' Everything else in the world was different from this central 'I', because it was subject to Cartesian doubt, and could be imagined away as a delusion under the spotlight of radical scepticism. Mind and body were thus two completely different kinds of substance, mysteriously (and implausibly) conjoined through the rarified spirituous Pineal gland. Other animals than man were totally physical, moving mechanically, according to mechanical laws, incapable of thought or feeling. Man alone was essentially a rational, thinking being, conscious of his own self, and distinct from his body. Christianity, and especially the Platonism that exercised so powerful an influence on the early Fathers, encouraged such a belief. For Platonism taught that the soul of man was a temporary inhabitant of the body, longing to escape its limitations and tribulations, but, at least in aspiration, in control of the body while its sojourn on earth lasted. I, my rational thinking self, am like a leaseholder, with full rights of possession of the habitation which for the time being I occupy.

By now, however, it is hard to defend such dualism. For one thing, we cannot escape our post-Darwinian place in history. We, most of us, have no inclination to divorce ourselves completely, as Descartes did, from other animals. We know how much of our DNA, out of which our life is built up, is shared by non-human living organisms. Moreover we know, though still very imperfectly, how our brains function with our central nervous system, to give rise to physical feelings, emotions, memories and thoughts (all of which were classed by Descartes as '*pensés*', 'thoughts', that which I discover by introspection and which can be articulated in language). And brains are physical objects. For me, therefore, my body, including my brain, is my way of being-in-the-world, my entrée into the universe. I cannot think of it as one of my possessions, just one among others.

English law confirms this common-sense view. If my grandson comes in, pouring blood, and says he has been mugged, we know that mugging is made up of two elements, assault and theft. He has lost a tooth in the attack, but he does not count this as theft. He has also lost his mobile phone; and this was the theft element of the crime. He did not own his tooth in the same way as he owned his phone. In the case *R v Bentham*,[5] the Appellate Judges in the House of Lords (now the Supreme Court) considered whether a person who concealed his hand under his jacket to give the impression that he was concealing a firearm there was rightly charged with being in possession of an imitation firearm, contrary to subsection 17(2) of the Firearms Act 1968. The original trial judge held that a person could be convicted on those facts, and the Court of Appeal upheld the decision. The House of Lords, however, reversed the decision of the Court of Appeal, and quashed the conviction. Lord Justice Bingham, summing up, said 'One cannot possess something which is not separate and distinct from oneself. An unsevered hand or finger is part of oneself. A person's hand or fingers are not a thing'. The jurist J.E. Penner also argues that all property rights are rights to things that are only contingently connected to an individual and are not intrinsic to a human being. The idea of separability is central to his concept of what constitutes a 'thing', and may therefore be the subject of ownership.[6]

The case of a severed hand or finger is, by implication, a different matter; and this is the second kind of case I must briefly consider (though only to rule it out from detailed examination), for it has become extremely controversial in recent years. In the invented case of my grandson, above, it could be argued that his tooth, once it had been knocked out, became his property over which he had rights of ownership, as much as over his mobile phone. The legal question, which is now much disputed, is this: who owns biological material, such as a tooth, derived from a particular individual who is its source? This question may arise, whether the material is a severed limb, an organ, a blood sample, or a sample of DNA. All such biological material has become enormously important in medical research, in organ transplant and in research carried out commercially by pharmaceutical companies, as well as in criminal investigations and in issues about proof of paternity. The question is whether the source of the biological material can claim ownership rights over

---

5 [2005]UKHL18; [2005]WLR1057(HL).

6 See J.E. Penner, *The Idea of Property* (Oxford University Press, Oxford 1997) p. 111.

it, or whether the ownership lies with the individual or institution that actually holds the material, or whether each case must be judged separately, in the light of the circumstances. It would have been reasonable to hope that, in English law, such issues would have been settled once and for all by the passage of the Human Tissue Act in 2004. However, the uncertainty remains.

The Human Tissue Act came onto the Statute Book following two scandals, chiefly involving the Children's Hospital in Liverpool (Alder Hey), and the Bristol Royal Infirmary (though other NHS – National Health Service – hospitals were later shown also to have been involved) where large numbers of body parts, whole organs and tissue, taken from children who had died in hospital, had been retained without the knowledge or consent of their parents, and, at Alder Hey especially, for no apparent purpose or use. Here a particular, possibly unbalanced, doctor from the Netherlands seems to have been responsible for most of the collection and retention of the organs. The outrage was enormous, and, to the embarrassment of the Church, often led to a demand for a second or even a third burial service, as a body part came to light. It was important to many of the parents that their child should have been buried, as they had supposed, complete and intact. 'How can she love us from heaven without a heart?' one mother wrote, in a letter to a newspaper.

However irrational the response, the scandals had a serious effect on medical research and organ transplant, donors and, especially the relatives of potential donors refusing to trust so flawed a system enough to give the necessary consent. It was natural, therefore, that the new legislation should concentrate mainly on the matter of consent, especially consent from relatives for the use of body parts, and should not directly address the question of who, if anyone, owns them.

The second reason for the failure of the Act to address the problem of ownership is the long tradition in English Common Law (and in Australia, Canada and the USA) that complete dead bodies can have no owners. This principle is known as the 'No Property Principle', and can be traced back at least to the mid-seventeenth century. At that time Sir Edward Coke, in his book *The Institutes of the Laws of England*,[7] gave an agreeable explanation. He argued that the No Property

[7] E. Coke, *The Third Part of the Institutes of the Laws of England* (London, 4th edn 1669) vol. III p. 203.

Principle was self-evident, if one thought about the etymology of the word 'cadaver' (corpse). 'Cadaver' was short for '*Caro Data Vermibus*' ('flesh given to the worms'). If it had been given to the worms it could not belong to anyone else. Obviously, this bogus etymology contains no truth whatsoever. But despite its extremely dubious derivation, the principle survived, so that William Blackstone, a century or so later, stated, of grave-robbers, that 'stealing the corpse itself, which has no owner, though a matter of great indecency, is no felony, unless some of the grave-clothes be stolen with it'.[8]

The debates in the House of Commons and the House of Lords on the Human Tissue Bill make no reference to property or ownership. It is true that consent to keep or use might imply ownership, as I might give consent that you should drive my car when yours has broken down. But it need not do so. I must consent to a surgeon's cutting up my body, but this is an appeal to the principle of autonomy rather than that of ownership, since we have seen that I do not own my body. And it seems that the emphasis on consent in the context of retaining body parts is an extension of this same principle, parents exercising autonomy on behalf of their children, as is always the case. The principle of autonomy, or patient choice, which in the last twenty years or so has formed a major part of medical ethics, and is taught like a gospel to medical students, dominated the thinking behind the Human Tissue Act, so the question of ownership was forgotten.

Some years before the passage in England of the Human Tissue Act 2004, however, the courts in the USA were forced to confront the problem of ownership of body parts head on. This was in the case of *Moore v Regents of the University of California*, a case which is often taken by jurists and bioethicists as the starting point of any debate about the ownership of body parts. In 1976 John Moore visited the UCLA medical centre after he had been diagnosed as suffering from leukaemia. There the diagnosis was confirmed, and his doctor, Doctor David Golde, recommended that his spleen be removed. Moore signed a written consent form for the splenectomy which was duly carried out. There was nothing in the consent form that referred to the future use of the spleen when it had been removed. Over the next seven years, while Moore frequently returned to the medical

---

[8] W. Blackstone, *Commentaries on the Laws of England* (Clarendon, Oxford 9th edn 1783) vol. IV p. 2.

centre to give samples of blood, blood serum and cells from skin and bone-marrow, Dr Golde and his assistant, Dr Shirley Quan, were attempting to establish a cell-line from the cells of Moore's spleen which were particularly useful, since they overproduced certain lymphokines, that is, substances related to white blood cells and activated by contact with antibodies. They thus played an important role in the immune system. By 1979, Golde and Quan had succeeded in producing a cell-line from the spleen. This meant that they had virtually turned the cells from Moore's spleen into stem cells that could reproduce themselves for ever, and be used either for direct transplant into other damaged tissue, or for the creation of drugs for enhancing the immune system. The process that they had discovered to establish the cell-line was therefore of enormous potential value, both scientific and commercial. In 1984 the University of California was granted a patent for the process, and for methods of using the cell-line that had been set up, whose commercial value was estimated as $3 billion over a period of six years. The Regents of the University immediately entered into agreements with a genetic research institute and a pharmaceutical company, granting rights of access to the cell-line (which, incidentally, was one of the few cell-lines in the United States that survived the axe of George W. Bush more than a decade later, when he, absurdly, called a halt to all stem-cell research, but allowed existing cell-lines to remain).

Although Moore had frequently attended the medical centre since his first visit in 1976, it was not until 1983, just before the granting of the patent, that he was asked to sign a consent form that would permit continued research on his spleen, which referred to rights that he had over the use of the spleen. He was requested to hand over the form with his signature to the Regents of the University. However, he refused to sign. He then brought an action, naming five defendants, the two doctors, the Regents of the University and the two companies to whom rights had been sold. He named no less than thirteen causes of action, of which only one, the tort of conversion, was taken up by the courts. The tort of conversion is 'wrongfully dealing with a person's goods in a way that constitutes a denial of the owner's rights or an assertion of rights inconsistent with the owner's'.[9] In such a case the plaintiff has specifically to

---

[9] *Concise Dictionary of Law* (Oxford University Press, Oxford 1983).

prove ownership. This meant that Moore had to prove that he was the owner of his spleen which had been removed with consent seven years earlier. Moore lost his case at the first (Superior) court, and proceeded to Appeal. The Appeal Court, by a majority, upheld the appeal, but failed to establish that they did so on the grounds that Moore owned his spleen. They contented themselves with asserting that he had rights of control over the uses to which his body parts should be put, and also, rather oddly, that to deny this kind of control would constitute an 'invasion of privacy'. (The concept of privacy is closely connected with that of ownership in other contexts, as we shall see; but it seems somewhat bizarre in the particular case of Moore's spleen, which was no longer part of his body, and with which he had had no connection for years.) The Regents of the University and the other defendants appealed against this judgment, and the Supreme Court of the State of California reversed the decision of the Court of Appeal, by a majority decision. The majority held that though Moore might have a case against Dr Golde for failing to get his informed consent for the use of his spleen, he had no case in tort of conversion, since he did not retain any proprietory interest in his spleen, once it had been removed: it was, in short, of no further use to him.

But this is surely to beg the question. What is needed is a decision as to who owns the spleen at the moment when it is removed. I gave birth to one of my children in a small nursing home where I could look out into the garden and see the two nurses who ran it (dishearteningly called Nurse Payne and Sister Screech) digging the placentae of their patients into their rose beds. I remember feeling mild resentment. I thought my roses too might have benefited. But whether or not I had used the placenta to fertilise my garden has no bearing on the question whether it was indeed mine (later I learned that, at least in some American birth centres, the women are sent home each with her placenta in a plastic bag, plainly as part of her belongings). However this may be, we should ask whether Moore's case would have been stronger in law if he had happened himself to be a research scientist in the field of human cells. For he would then have had a continued ownership interest in the biological material. But the law surely cannot turn on such an accident as the profession of the patient. One of the dissenting judges at the Californian Supreme Court held that because patients should have a right to control the subsequent use of what had been parts of their body, this right should be protected by conversion law. The other dissenting judge simply denied the truth of the proposition upon which the judgment of the majority appeared to rest, namely that the concept of ownership could have no application to detached body parts. After all, in cases of transplant, an organ can be given as a gift. One cannot be a donor unless one owns what is donated.

In the end the decision against Moore's claim to participate in the profits derived from his spleen seemed to rest on matters of policy rather than of strict principles of justice: it was held by the majority of judges that, though in some circumstances it might be appropriate to claim ownership of body parts, in the case of Moore and others in a similar situation, the effect on medical research would be disastrous if his claim were allowed. The incentive to research would be diminished if profits were to be shared, and thus so drastically reduced. The judgment seems to have been pragmatic; but it may serve as a precedent that will ultimately determine disputes about the ownership of detached body parts and tissue. No one can doubt that they are 'things'.[10]

There is another alleged reason for a resistance to the notion that body parts should be classified as property, owned by the person of whose body they are part. If they were so classified, it would be open to anyone to sell one of his kidneys. At present this is not lawful either in the UK or in the USA. If ownership by living people of separate, or separable, body parts were permitted, the right to dispose of them by sale would be included in the package of rights that belong to the owner. It is widely held that it would not be in the public interest to change the law in this respect, since it might lead to the exploitation of the most poverty-stricken members of society, who would risk their health and even their lives by giving up one of their kidneys for profit.

Most kidneys for transplant are acquired either from relatives of the patient in need who are of matching blood group, or from newly dead corpses, especially of those who have been killed in road or other accidents. But such a source is chancy, and subject to

---

[10] For a full critical examination of the Moore case, and many other cases, with all the relevant references, see R. Hardcastle, *Law and the Human Body* (Oxford University Press, Oxford 2007) especially pp. 65–71, the source from which, as I gratefully acknowledge, I have learned most of the facts of Moore.

disastrous delays, if consent has to be obtained from relatives (few victims of accidents carry donor cards). Very few people donate a kidney, as they may donate blood, to an unknown recipient, out of generalised benevolence. The result is a great shortage of organs for transplant and a long waiting list of patients on dialysis, many of whom die before they reach the top of the list. There are those, therefore, who believe that a regulated NHS-run market in kidneys should be established, which would save lives and save the cost to the health service of treatment and dialysis.[11] Public opinion seems generally hostile to such a change, partly, no doubt, because of the risk of exploitation, but partly, I suspect, out of a kind of squeamish distaste for an open market in body parts, though it is known that people, for example in India, do sell their kidneys for cash. There seems to be some redeeming virtue in donation, even posthumous donation, rather than sale. But we must recognise that this is an issue that can only grow more urgent.

Problems similar to those of donated organs arise more and more frequently in the case of donated eggs and sperm for assisted fertilisation. Once again, the very idea of donation suggests ownership of what is given; yet, perhaps because these 'things' are so nearly human beings, so essential to any resulting human embryo, there is an understandable, though not wholly rational, squeamishness about setting up a market in which such goods may be sold competitively. As usual in Europe, the matter is settled by regulation and convention.

As Rohan Hardcastle concludes in the book already referred to,[12] the present state of the law regarding rights over separated body parts, including cells and cell-lines, is confused. He argues that the basis should be ownership, and that ownership should lie with the source of the biological material, as John Moore had claimed in the 1980s. The owner could then be asked to donate the material, or alternatively would have to be paid for its use. The cost involved to medical research institutions and pharmaceutical companies would, he admits, have to be carefully estimated. Account

---

[11] See, for example, an article published online by the British Medical Association on 3 August 2011 by Dr Sue Eabbitt Roff, a renologist from the University of Dundee. The BMA itself made it known that they would not support such a change in the law.

[12] Op. cit., pp. 293–4.

would have to be taken, for example, of the number of women who, in the euphoria of childbirth, might voluntarily donate their placenta and umbilical cord, rich sources of stem cells (though of a limited variety), for use in research or therapy. However, my guess is that the cost to research, academic or directly commercial, would be enormous, and ever-increasing with the discovery of new techniques in the field of cell manipulation and cell transplantation. I believe that the step from consent to the use of biological material to ownership of it by the source will be taken, if at all, with extreme reluctance, whatever the demands of clarity or natural justice.

Hardcastle acknowledges that such a change in the law, to give sources clear ownership rights over their organs, might give rise to an open market for the sale of kidneys, rather than a market regulated by NHS commissioners, and demand for kidney transplant might be such as to make prices unaffordable by the NHS. But that would not necessarily follow. All ownership is subject to the limitation that the use of the property must not be damaging (for example, if I live in London, I may not cut down a tree in my garden and make a bonfire of it); and it could, as we have seen, be argued that to put the poor at risk of self-harm would be to damage not only individuals but also a society which aims for at least a show of equality. Some system of cap on prices demanded might be enforced.

In any case, at present, despite the Human Tissue Act and the one-time existence of a body entrusted with overseeing the implementation of the Act, the status of biological material in England is unclear (and the position is no better in the USA and Australia). As we have seen, separation from a living body turns biological material into a 'thing', capable of being the subject of ownership, or property. But the question of whose property it may be, its source or those who would use it, is subject to an important provision. It is held that the application of 'work and skill' to the 'thing', whether spleen or placenta, serves to create property rights and ownership for the person whose work and skill is employed. For the skill is held to change the original 'thing' in question into another, different 'thing'. This new thing could be a permanent cell-line, for example, or even, according to the first appearance of the principle,[13] a part of a collection, or a

[13] In Australian law: *Doodeward v Spence* 1908.

teaching aid. The work and skill in the latter case would be the work of fixing and preserving the thing in question, which may indeed have been a laborious process.

The Australian case, an appeal against a judgment of the Supreme Court of New South Wales, is highly instructive, if somewhat macabre. In 1868 a woman gave birth in New Zealand to a baby with two heads. The baby was still-born, and the doctor arrived after the birth, and took the dead baby away and preserved it as 'a curiosity'. After his death in 1870, the preserved baby was sold at auction, and came into the possession of a Mr Doodeward. However the police came to hear of it, and a policeman (Spence) removed the preserved baby from its apparently legitimate owner, for it to be given a Christian burial, on the grounds that there can be no ownership of a corpse, but that it may be lawfully retained only between its death and its burial, in this case a period of forty years. Chief Justice Griffith held that the work and skill put in by the doctor who had first removed the dead baby had turned it into a thing different from a corpse; and that in any case, by analogy with the possession by students and teaching hospitals of skeletons or other anatomical parts of human bodies, the law must respect property rights over such material:

> It is idle to contend in these days that the possession of a mummy, or of a prepared skeleton, or of a skull or other parts of a human body is necessarily unlawful; if it is, the many valuable collections of anatomical and pathological specimens or preparations formed and maintained by scientific bodies, were formed and are maintained in violation of the law.

The Human Tissue Act 2004 gave ownership rights over whole mummified bodies or shrunken scalps to the original (mostly Aboriginal) sources and made it lawful for national museums, at that time prohibited by law from disposing of any of their holdings, to return them to their country of origin if requested to do so (a further exception has since been made for objects acquired by looting or forced sale from families persecuted by the Nazis between 1933 and 1945). But, as we have seen, this was not on the basis of work and skill having been applied to change the attributes of the 'things' but because consent had not been given to their being held in the museums in the first place. Nevertheless, however uncertain the 'work and skill' proviso is (and the eminent gynaecologist,

Lord Naren Patel, remarked in his speech in the second reading debate of the Human Tissue Bill on 22 July 2004 that the interpretation of case law in this matter was far from straightforward), it may possibly afford a way out of the difficulty, described above, of allowing ownership to the sources of separated body parts. For it could be argued that the undoubtedly skilful surgery required to remove a spleen or a tumour had transformed the 'thing' that had been part of the patient's body into a different 'thing', a cluster of cells useful for research or educational purposes.

The ownership of body parts is, as I have said, an issue that is not only historically complicated, but likely to become increasingly contentious with the advance of sophisticated microbiological research. Yet I shall say no more about it in what follows. My consideration of ownership will, from now on, follow a different track. As I have explained, I want to explore what it is actually like to own something, and especially to own a part of one's immediate environment, a house, a garden, two acres and a cow; in short, what it is like to own a property. This might, in currently fashionable usage, be described as an exploration of the *existential* nature of ownership.

I shall consider what difference it makes to one's attitude to a 'thing' whether or not one owns it, and what difference it makes to one's responsibilities, or one's *feeling of* responsibility, for the maintenance, wellbeing or preservation of that thing. (Incidentally this close connection between ownership and responsibility is reflected in the currently common use of the word 'ownership' actually to mean 'responsibility'. Thus the chairman of a board may say to a board member 'I will give you ownership of that project'.)

We must also examine to what extent the feeling that something belongs to me and not to you (surely a most ancient and instinctive feeling) may be transferred to common or joint ownership, when the 'thing' belongs to *us* and not to *them*. Is it possible to conceive of something that is owned by everyone in the world, or is this a contradiction? And are there things (like human beings, alive or even perhaps dead, as we have seen) that we wish that nobody may own, such as wild animals and birds, and wilderness?

There is no doubt that the concept of what is mine and not yours is deeply embedded in the psychology of the individual. But it is also a political concept of great consequence, embedded as it is in law and therefore in the idea of civil society. Such ideas, of course, are not static, but change throughout history. But philosophers, from Plato onwards, have sought to clarify the concepts of political life by going back to their origins, or rather to their imagined origins, when life was simpler, and when no political institutions yet existed. It is to such imagined origins of society, and thus of property that we must now turn.

2. Origins of society and property

In the discussion of the ownership of detached body parts, we encountered the idea that the work and skill that a skilled worker (or microbiologist) puts into an object to transform it, or to make it into something else, entitle him to claim ownership of that newly changed object. Such an idea is far from new. The institution of patenting was established to regulate and protect such claims, but we can go further back than that. In the psalms of David, over and over again, we find the assumption that what you have made is your own: 'The earth is the Lord's and all that therein is: the compass of the world, and they that dwell therein. For He hath founded it upon the seas, and prepared it upon the floods'.[1] 'It is He that hath made us and not we ourselves; we are His people and the sheep of His pasture',[2] 'In His hand are all the corners of the earth; and the strength of the hills is His also. The sea is His and He made it; and His hand prepared the dry land'.[3] The creator of the universe who made it with his own hand is, in virtue of that very fact, the rightful owner of that universe.

It is, after all, a naturally intelligible idea. Birds build their nests and they defend them, and the eggs and chicks for whose protection they were made, against predators; they often return to the same nest year after year, adding bits to it and improving it. The nests are theirs and they made them: their nests are, accordingly, their property, though they do not have the benefit of laws to protect their possession. And there is no doubt of the work and skill that went into the building of the nests of most birds. Birds are thus an example of what Jean-Paul Sartre refers to as a 'natural symbol':[4] in our perception of the world they are immediately understood as standing for the ownership of property.

---

1 Psalm 24 vv 1 and 2.

2 Psalm 100 v 2.

3 Psalm 95 vv 4 and 5.

4 J.-P. Sartre, *Being and Nothingness*, Part IV, Hazel Barnes (tr.) (Philosophical Library, New York 1948).

John Locke, the English philosopher who may be thought of as the founding father of the British empirical tradition, published his Two Treatises on Civil Government in 1690. The first was specifically directed to the demolition of the theory of Divine Right of Kings, a right that, it was claimed, derived from inheritance, kings, all of them, being descended from Adam. Locke, who was a deeply religious man, held that not only was the supposition that the lineage of all kings could be traced back to our first forefather absurd, but, even if it could be so traced, this would not give them absolute power, as those who upheld the divine right claimed. For it is in any case false that fathers have complete authority over their children once they are grown up. Worse than this, Locke argued, to suggest that one human being could rightfully exercise such power over his subjects was sacrilegious. It was nothing short of blasphemy to suggest that any human ruler, however close his relationship with the first man might prove to be, could claim absolute power over his people. Locke never wavered from the belief that God and only God, the creator, could claim such power.

This, then, was the destructive one of the two treatises, the preliminary 'clearing away of the brushwood', to use Locke's own metaphor. It may seem sad to us that Locke took as his target a keen defender of the divine right of the monarchy, Sir Robert Filmer, rather than Thomas Hobbes, whose powerful political writing, especially his *Leviathon*, is well worth studying and taking issue with today, as Sir Robert's *Patriarcha* (published after his death, in 1689) is certainly not, except as a curiosity in the history of ideas. But, in Locke's words it 'made such a noise on its coming abroad' that it was probably at the time a more satisfactory enemy to demolish than Hobbes's *Leviathan* (published in 1651) which in any case, though justifying absolute sovereignty, did not argue for any divine right of the sovereign to rule, but for the consent of those who were subjects, consent that had been given in an original contract.

The second treatise, published along with the first in 1690, was, unlike the first, constructive, and devoted to exploring the proper relation between king and people, all alike subject to the absolute power of the divine creator. The second Treatise was much read, and was to prove highly influential on future history. But the ideas it propounded were not particularly original. They were widely shared and discussed thirty years before the treatise was written. A political theory virtually the same as Locke's lay behind the development of the British constitution, following the restoration of the monarchy in 1660, and the expulsion of James II in 1688. What Locke did, in this treatise, was to supply theoretical justification for both the restoration and the expulsion of a monarch, ex post facto. The theory in fact seemed thoroughly vindicated by the prosperity following the Restoration. Further ahead, because of its wide acceptance, it was to be the origin of the American Declaration of Independence, the birth of the American constitution and the Bill of Rights. In general, it was the philosophical backdrop to British colonial expansion long after Locke's death.

The full title of the second treatise is *An Essay concerning the True Original Extent and End of Civil Government*. It is an accurate description. Locke was interested equally in the question of the limits of the powers of sovereign government, and in its purpose. The theory is built upon the popular contemporary hypothesis of a 'state of nature', out of which grew an 'original contract', according to which people voluntarily handed over their natural autonomy, a crucial part of their humanity, to a chosen ruler, giving him the authority to legislate. But this authority was limited by the purpose for which it was established. The purpose of setting up a government was for the wellbeing of the people who chose to set it up. If this purpose was not fulfilled, then those people might properly overthrow the government, and agree to form another.

As a student, like many others, I used to be critical of any political theory that rested on the hypothesis of an original contract, arguing that something presented as history, but supported by no sort of evidence, could provide no firm foundation for an account of government, either of its origins or its present status and authority. I was inclined to hold a pistol to Locke's head, and demand 'Did it actually happen this way? Yes or No?'. And if the answer was 'No' or 'Don't know', then the story of the original contract must be abandoned as useless. I, as so often, found myself much more inclined to follow the scepticism of David Hume, a generation later, who rejected, with his usual self-protective irony (which always managed to avoid a positive declaration of atheism), both the theory that the right to make laws was divinely ordained, and the theory that originally people promised or contracted to obey a ruler. And I still believe that, as he proposed, historically, the cooperation and regard for rights to life and property that are essential to civil society were probably of slow growth, and became a matter of convention, or a mixture of convention, habit, and self-interest, before needing to be formalised and becoming a constitution within which legislative powers and procedures were instituted, and courts established for the enforcement of law. We know, after all, that there have been certain key moments, when progress has been made from the more to the less primitive. An example is the establishing of the court of the Areopagiticus in sixth-century BC Athens, celebrated by Aeschylus in the *Eumenides*, when the private duty of a family to avenge the death of its members throughout generations, was replaced by the public impartiality of the criminal law, so as to bring the vendetta to an end.

Hume opened his Essay On the First Principles of Government[5] with these words:

> Nothing appears more surprising to those who consider human affairs with a philosophical eye than the easiness with which the many are governed by the few; and the implicit submission with which men resign their own sentiments and passions to those of their rulers. When we inquire by what means this wonder is effected, we shall find that, as Force is always on the side of the governed, the governors have nothing to support them but opinion.

And the opinion of the vast majority of people, who submit to be governed by a few, is that it is in their interest to do so. They need the protection of both their lives and their property that nothing but established legislation and established courts can afford. He thus agreed with Locke that, in general terms, government rests and must always have rested on the consent of those who are governed. But consensual interaction does not entail a contract: 'Two men, who pull the oars of a boat, do it by an agreement or convention, tho' they have never given promises to each other'.[6] They simply learn by experience that mutual collaboration works.

Hume's theory is thus basically utilitarian: people learn to act in a way that produces the best consequences for the largest number. His theory is also extremely conservative, in that things would really have to get very bad indeed before there could be justification (in terms of a better outcome) for overthrowing arrangements and

---

5 David Hume, *Essays Moral, Political and Literary* (1741) Essay IV.

6 Hume, *A Treatise of Human Nature* (1741) Book III, part II, section II.

institutions to which people have grown accustomed over the years and to which they have developed a loyalty, and a 'habit of obedience' which itself contributes to stability.

However, though I am more than ever convinced, like Hume, of the power of history in securing constitutional stability, I now believe that myths need not be literally true to be useful, even explanatory, for those who understand that this is what they are, and do not take them to be attempts at historical accuracy. People may accept myths as natural metaphors, like the 'ownership' of their nests by the birds which made them. And the ideal embodied in Locke's myth is this: that a civil society is founded so that people should be able to live in it secure in their life, in at least some of their liberty and in their property; and that if a government fails to secure these ends for the people subjected to that government, then it rests with the people to strip it of power. Authority lasts only so long as the purpose of government, namely the overall good of the people, and the furthering of their interests is fulfilled.

The ideal embodied in this mythical contract has been of enormous importance to Britain, and perhaps of even more importance to America. Locke took over and developed a narrative which was not his invention, but which had been told in various forms since the time of Plato, and which was developed especially by Aquinas and later Thomists. In Locke's version, the original contract, the beginning of civil society, coincided with the beginning of the idea of property and that of ownership. Human beings were turning from hunter-gatherers (not Locke's word, of course) to agricultural creatures who built houses, domesticated animals and sowed crops, rather than living nomadically, off what they could scavenge, and without the idea of ownership, as opposed to mere possession.

Chapter V of the second treatise is entitled 'Of Property'. Here Locke sets out his account of how the rights of private property came into being. He starts by quoting Psalm 115: 'Ye are the blessed of the Lord: who made heaven and earth. All the whole heavens are the Lord's: the earth hath He given to the children of men'.[7] This, according to Locke, meant that the earth was the *common property* of all mankind. It had belonged to God, as his creation, and he had given it to his people to be theirs. So the question must be raised how

[7] Psalm 115 vv 15 and 16.

individual men could come into individual possession of parts of the earth, and this without any formal allocation by God of the parts between them. Locke answers the question thus:

> God who hath given the world to men in common, hath also given them reason, to make use of it to the best advantage of life and convenience. The earth and all that is therein is given to men for the support and comfort of their being. And though all the fruits it naturally produces and beasts it feeds, belong to mankind in common, as they are produced by the spontaneous hand of Nature, and nobody has originally a private dominion exclusive of the rest of mankind in any of them as they are thus in their natural state, yet being given for the use of men, there must of necessity be a means to appropriate them one way or another before they can be of any use or at all beneficial to any particular men.[8]

Locke argues that the means in question, which is both commanded by God and demanded by reason, is the labour that a man puts into the products of nature.

> Though the earth and all inferior creatures be common to all men, yet every man has a 'property' in his own 'person'. This nobody has any right to but himself. The 'labour' of his body and the 'work' of his hands, we may say, are properly his. Whatever, then, he removes out of the state that nature has provided and left it in, he has mixed his labour with it and joined it to something that is his own, and thereby makes it his property. It being by him removed from the common state Nature placed it in, it hath by this labour something annexed to it that excludes the common right of other men. For this 'labour' being the unquestionable property of the labourer, no man but he can have a right to what that is once joined to.[9]

When Locke says that every man has a 'property' in his own body, he is not saying that every man owns his own body, or has a legal right to its possession in the sense discussed in the first chapter. He is, rather, playing on the fact that the word 'property' is equivocal (and was more obviously so in seventeenth-century usage than it is now). Besides the sense in which it is now most commonly used, of one's estate, goods and chattels, it also had a sense derived from Aristotelian logic, meaning a characteristic that is essential to a person or thing (as opposed to 'an accident'). So, in the Book of

---

8 Second Treatise Chapter V para. 25.
9 Ibid., para. 26.

Common Prayer, we pray to God 'Whose property is Always to have Mercy'. For each man, his 'person', that is his bodily self, is essential to his existence. Without it he would not be who he is. Being uniquely essential to him, it does not belong to anybody else. And here Locke effects a smooth transition from one sense of the word 'property' to the other by saying, of the property that a man has in his own person 'And this nobody has any right to but himself'. For the question of rights is relevant not to the Aristotelian sense of 'property', but only to the more usual modern sense, in which the word means 'what he owns'. This is Locke's attempt to find a place for property rights that can be shown to precede civil society, that is within a social group that formed a kind of community before the positive law which now protects the ownership of property came into existence. As we have seen, the law, when it did come into existence, denied ownership to an individual of his own body. So Locke's initial assumption, that a man's labour gives him a claim to ownership through ownership of his body, is shaky at best, and rests on an equivocation, an ambiguity in the word 'property'.

However, though it involves a bit of sleight of hand, Locke's argument has a certain plausibility which it retains, as we have also seen, even to this day, as evidenced by the 'work and skill' assumptions that surfaced in the discussion of the ownership of body parts in the last chapter. For 'work and skill' seem in some circumstances to transform something, tissue or body part, into something different, a 'thing' that can be owned by the person who has exercised the work and the skill upon it. So the labour a man puts in to cultivating what was a part of wild nature converts that piece of earth into something else, a field or a pasture, in other words something that is recognisably a piece of landed property.

In his account of the origin of property, Locke was speaking of an imagined time when the world was sparsely populated, land seemed boundless and there was no situation of scarcity or competition. And he recognised that these were the conditions assumed in his account. For at the end of paragraph 26, quoted above, he adds that a man's right to claim ownership of that with which he has mixed his labour applies 'at least where there is enough and as good left in common for others'. In this idyllic world no reasonable person would want to claim as his property more than he could himself cultivate and use for his family's needs; and he could rest assured that in taking as much as he needed, he would not be depriving anybody else of anything. There was plenty for all. 'Nobody could think himself injured by the drinking of another man, though he took a good draught, who had a whole river of the same water left him to quench his thirst'.[10] This suggests a situation exceedingly unlike that in which we live today, where scarcity of water is one of the most serious threats to survival in many parts of the world. But this assumption of plenty was never more natural than at the time when Locke wrote, and whole, apparently limitless lands were being discovered.

Locke's view of human nature, as well as of world resources, was essentially optimistic. God had given reason as a part of human nature; and reason would countervail against vices such as greed, envy or selfishness. In this rosy view Locke was very unlike his older contemporary, Thomas Hobbes, whose work Locke did not discuss. For Hobbes, the state of nature was a state of 'war of all against all' and there was no subduing the innate greed, selfishness and ambition of men, their 'restless pursuit of power after power', except by the contracting away of all their rights to self-government, into the hands of an absolute sovereign. But Locke's view of man's nature was derived from his firm faith (a faith not shared by the atheist Hobbes) in the benevolence of God, who had not only given to men the world he had made for them, but had also given them the intelligence by which they could work out the best way to improve it. In the state of nature men were both rational and industrious:

> God gave the world to men in common, but since He gave it them for their benefit and the greatest conveniencies of life they were capable to draw from it, it cannot be supposed that it should always remain common and uncultivated. He gave it to the use of the industrious and rational . . . not to the fancy or covetousness of the quarrelsome and contentious. He that had as much left for his improvement as was already taken up, needed not complain, ought not to meddle with what was already improved by another's labour; if he did, it is plain he desired the benefit of another's pains which he had no right to.[11]

As I have said, Locke admitted that things had radically changed since the beginning of civil society, and especially since the introduction of money, through the conventional value of which property could be bought and sold. For the fact that actual materials for food

---

10 Ibid., para. 32.
11 Ibid., para. 33.

did not last put a limit to what a man could claim as his own. If he accumulated more apples than he could eat and let them rot, he was taking more than his share. Someone else should have claimed ownership of them, who could use them. But since metal or diamonds were durable, he could accumulate piles of them for as long as he liked, and nobody else was necessarily deprived. The value assigned to these durable things, undoubtedly 'things' that could be owned, was purely artificial, nothing immediately to do with their value as a means to sustaining life. And so, Locke thought, began the exchange of property, change of ownership secured by monetary exchange, and with this began disparity of wealth, the employment of people to cultivate land other than their own (and whose labour mixed with the land certainly gave them no rights of ownership), and the whole apparatus of modern agriculture and indeed industry. For Locke's mythical state of nature was a commonwealth founded on what he believed to be the natural equality of men. None was much more powerful than another, though some were doubtless better at cultivating the land and providing for their families. And since they were all so equally industrious and decent, none was an employer or an employee. Each worked for himself and his dependants.

As I have said, Locke recognised that times had changed, that the world was far more populous, and that what we should call 'capitalism' was now thoroughly established, with the accumulation of wealth and the employment by landowners of non-landowning labourers. He nevertheless noted that in central Spain it was still possible to earn possession of waste land by cultivating it, and that people on the whole were grateful rather than envious when this was done. Here was something more like a state of nature.

In general, however, whatever might happen in remote and primitive parts of the world, we must assume that Locke was quite aware that, in talking of an original contract, he was accepting a current, broadly metaphorical, way of referring to what seemed to political theorists to be the salient facts about human nature: that man is, in Aristotle's words, a political animal, whose life is necessarily to be lived in a Polis, or a state, of some kind or other, and that in such a state, individual men would establish families, and own property. As Locke recognised, ownership itself is, in the broadest sense, a political concept. Locke was convinced that, whether in history or in myth, human beings were essentially rational, could think for themselves and had worked out a way by which, in their own long-term interests, they and their property could be protected by law and legitimate institutions.

It is remarkable that probably the most powerful and long-enduring aspect of the myth of the state of nature, and the original contract, as Locke propounded it, is its assertion that men are naturally equal. Realistically, if one thinks for a moment, it is plain that they are not. As with other animals, some are sickly, some healthy, for a start. In fact, there are only two senses in which men can be said to be born equal. One is that they are equal in the eyes of God, all equally His creatures (and this Locke certainly believed); the other is that they are equal under the law. But justice, or impartiality, as Hume argued, is an 'artificial' virtue, nothing to do with nature, but the result of human devising, arising out of that very civil society that the original contract was supposed to set up. Equality in this sense is not only artificial, in Hume's sense, but fragile, something to be prized and protected by society and part of the very concept of the rule of law. And the loss of such equality before the law, or its threatened loss, would be one of the causes that would, in Locke's view, be justification for the overthrow of a monarch. Yet here is Thomas Jefferson, well-versed in Locke's philosophy, and writing nearly a century after Locke, declaring 'We hold these truths to be self-evident that all men are created equal'. This can be nothing but a reference to their equality in the eyes of their creator; and it may seem astonishing in the twenty-first century that such a proposition be proclaimed to be self-evident.

To return, however, to the question of ownership: as an historian, Locke must have been well aware of the long process of land enclosure that had been going on around him, patchily, but steadily, since feudal times. Before enclosure, most land around villages (and that was most land) had in fact been cultivated in a manner not unlike that which Locke had envisaged in the state of nature. Fields were very large and were divided, by common agreement, into strips of which each farmer had several to plough and sow, leaving some fallow in turn. The strips were not divided from one another except by ditches. Each farmer cultivated enough for the needs of his own household. Apart from the land in the possession of feudal manors, much of the rest of the land was common, and on such common land villagers could graze their cattle freely. Then there was forest land where they could also graze their cattle and from which they could supply themselves with wood for building and fuel. They were not permitted to use axes to cut down trees, but to gather only 'by hook or crook' what was enough for their needs. There were numerous different codes of behaviour; and enclosure itself took different forms in different parts of the country. Most usual perhaps was the enclosure within hedges of smaller fields within the large open fields, though in the north country handmade stone walls were favoured above hedges. Parts of forests, where the soil was not too poor, were enclosed, and turned into use for arable or pasture; and free grazing of cattle in forest land was often restricted, in order to preserve the trees for timber. All these measures were in varying degrees unpopular with villagers, causing complaints and riots, sometimes led by those of the clergy who took up the interests of the poor. So the progress of enclosure was remarkably slow. We learn from Jane Austen that in the early nineteenth century enclosure was one of the regular topics of conversation among gentlemen after the ladies had withdrawn from dinner (*Sense and Sensibility* chapter XXXIV).

In fact Locke was right: the old system of owning only what you could use yourself could not survive, once the development of trade in corn had begun, and, even more importantly, the commerce in wool. Such trade had at first been a way that peasant farmers could make a bit of money on the side, but, long before Locke's day, it had developed into a major source of wealth.

Besides looking to feudal farm management to explain the origins of ownership, Locke had a more contemporary source. He turned naturally, as well, to the appropriation of property and the claims to ownership of the first settlers in America, over whose colonies his theories were in the end to have such great influence. As a schoolboy at Westminster, he must have been entirely familiar with romantic accounts of voyages to the New World, precarious adventures, and astonishing endurance.

It takes some effort of historical imagination to understand the outlook and motivation, and the expectations, of the early settlers of the New World, and indeed their motives and hopes were doubtless various. But there can be no doubt of the importance of the desire to escape from religious persecution; and therefore many of them will have believed that they would be obeying God's law in wishing not only to worship as they thought best, but also to acquire property and cultivate it as He intended. God had given them the earth to improve and enjoy. On landing in America, they found themselves in a state of nature within which there was apparently plenty of land for everyone, and no one need feel deprived if each took only enough for the needs of his own family and household. The whole extent of the country was unknown, and it seemed that there was endless wilderness to be cultivated, in everybody's interest. The injured parties, of course, were the native inhabitants, who were driven away from their settlements, or slaughtered ruthlessly by the new settlers. But the incomers could doubtless justify this by the reflection that the natives were neglecting the duty of improvement and cultivation which God had laid upon His creatures. And no doubt, if anyone felt pangs of guilt, they could comfort themselves by the thought that if only the natives would go quietly, there was probably enough for their needs further west. However, it has to be admitted that guilt about the sufferings of indigenous peoples was not to be a common moral sentiment for a long time, even among such God-fearing pioneers as the founding fathers in the New World, let alone among the ex-convicts in Australia.

By the eighteenth century, philosophical interest in the theoretical extent and limitations of the power of the sovereign seemed to diminish. In England the comparative stability of government, so surprisingly soon established after the Restoration, and surviving the removal of James II, meant that questions of the proper powers of the sovereign became less urgent, the myth of the original contract less relevant. And this was accompanied by a corresponding change in attitudes to the ownership of property. In Hume we find a view of ownership which is linked to more complex aspects of human nature than the mere need to provide for oneself and one's household, or even to secure the legitimacy of property-owning, and its protection by law.

Hume held that the relation between a human being and the world was determined not only by his senses and his reason, as Locke had supposed, but also by what he called his 'Passions', which were the desires, emotions and motives that cause him to act. This was an immensely significant addition to philosophical psychology, though not altogether new. Something like it was to be found implicitly in Aristotle, according to whom pure reason alone could not provide a motive, or cause one to take action. For that, what was needed was practical reason, a combination of desire, and an engagement in the actual world of means and ends.

Hume divided the passions into direct and indirect passions, the direct arising immediately from the perception of an object (as, say, fear, attraction or aversion may arise immediately from seeing or otherwise sensing an object), the indirect being more complicated. Among the indirect passions feature, most relevantly for our enquiry, pride and humility (or shame, as I shall call it). Pride is more than mere pleasure in an object; it is pleasure in the contemplation of it as connected with oneself in some identifiable way; similarly with the painful 'passion' of shame. I remember, many years ago, standing by the duck-pond in Oxford University Parks, with the philosopher, Peter Strawson, and some of our assorted children. A drake mallard repeatedly turned on a female and chased and harassed her, finally driving her protesting away from the group contending for the crusts our children were supplying. Peter said, most feelingly, 'I am *ashamed* of that duck'. I was pleased with the implication that, across species boundaries, he was identifying with the drake, perceiving him as an aggressively discourteous male, behaving badly to a poor dowdy female.

It does not matter, according to Hume, what precisely the connection is with the subject of pride or shame, as long as some connection or other can be found. So Peter Strawson found the connection between himself and the duck in the shared maleness. Most people experience pride or humiliation with regard to their children; some would extend these passions to embrace their parents, aunts and uncles and other more distant relatives. But the example to which Hume returns again and again is the relation of ownership. Near the beginning of the second book of the *Treatise of Human Nature* which is entitled Of the Passions, Hume lists some of the qualities of his mind or his body of which a man may be proud or of the absence of which he may be ashamed, qualities so closely connected to the man as to constitute his 'property' in the Aristotelian sense we have already noticed in Locke's usage. And he continues:

> But this is not all. The passions looking farther, comprehend whatever objects are in the least ally'd or related to us. Our country, family, children, relations, riches, houses, gardens, horses, dogs, cloaths; any of these may become a cause either of pride or of humility.[12]

Hume goes on to contrast pride with simple joy or pleasure which may be caused in us by a beautiful thing, which has no connection

[12] Hume, *A Treatise of Human Nature*, Book II, part I, section II.

with ourselves. And he notices as well that if something is enjoyed habitually, and by a very large number of people, such as health, although we may occasionally take especial pleasure from it when we are restored to health after illness, yet we do not usually take pride in it, because it is so widely shared. Pride is especially appropriate when it is caused in us by something which is ours and ours alone, as when we are actually its sole owner.[13] This observation leads Hume to the conclusion that 'The relation which is esteem'd the closest and which of all others produces the passion of pride is that of property'. For property is to be defined as 'such a relation betwixt a person and an object as permits him, but forbids any other, the free use and possession of it without violating the laws of equity and justice'.[14]

Here, then, is a pointer to one of the 'existential' features of property-owning of which we are in search: its closeness to ourselves, and only to ourselves. If it is mine, it is not yours. It is private, but if I love it and take care of it I am proud of it and may want to show it off. You may see it and admire it, but not have it, unless I choose to give it to you. In the following chapter I shall consider this feature in more detail, in connection with one form of property-owning, to which Hume constantly refers, the ownership of gardens. Here I hope clearly to illustrate the attitudes, emotions and motives, in short, in Hume's terminology, 'the Passions', that may be felt in the experience of ownership.

---

[13] Ibid., section VI.
[14] Ibid., section X.

3. Property, intimacy and privacy: gardening as ownership in action

In his book *Thoughtful Gardening*[1] Robin Lane Fox remarks that most people begin their serious gardening in middle age, when that other preoccupation and object of love, their children, have become less demanding of attention. This was not true of him: he fell in love with alpine plants when he was still at school, and he spent a gap year between school and university working in the Black Forest, apprenticed to an alpine expert. In consequence he is now not only a highly distinguished Greek historian, but the most enlightening and sympathetic, and certainly the most thoughtful, writer on gardening, who has responsibility not only for his own garden but for that of New College, Oxford, of which he is a Fellow. His suggestion that a preoccupation with gardening is in some way akin to, or a replacement for, a preoccupation with children would not seem in the least inapt to Hume. Both are matters of pride and shame, of often unrealistic hopes and plans, and therefore often consequent disappointment. But with one's children, uniquely, the relationship changes; they may still be a source of pride or shame, but they become one's equals as they grow up and detach themselves from one's plans and responsibilities (unless of course they are sadly unable to achieve such independence). This is why, though ours, they are not counted at any time among our possessions. They are not things. In this chapter I shall explore what it is like, and has in the past been like, to own and cultivate a garden. To garden is to take possession of and try to bring under your will and your design a particular defined plot of land, to tame an area that would otherwise be natural wilderness. In chapter 6, below, I shall explore the concept of wilderness itself, and why we cannot do without it. Some things must be left without owners. Now, however, I am concerned with what may often seem a

---

[1] Robin Lane Fox, *Thoughtful Gardening: Great Plants, Great Gardens, Great Gardeners* (Penguin Books, Harmondsworth 2013).

constant battle against wild nature, though, as we shall see, there are some happy gardeners who call a truce, and manage successfully to collaborate with nature on almost equal terms.

I shall start at a lowly level with a brief account of some of the gardens I have owned. I was a typical middle-aged starter; indeed I came to serious gardening later than most. I lived for the first 24 years of my life taking for granted that there was a large garden for me to enjoy, a source of intense pleasure as well as of delicious fruit and vegetables, a place to sit out of doors and read, but full of childhood memories of 'resting' in my pram, listening to music coming from the house and trains shunting in Winchester station down the hill, and later climbing trees, or hurtling over homemade obstacle courses on my bicycle. In the summer there were wonderful smells of roses and sweet peas, though these smells were best enjoyed in the house when the flowers had been freshly picked, and of mown grass. In the autumn, there were apples to pick and bonfire smells. I, of course, had no responsibility for any of this, any more than I had for the house itself. I did not own either house or garden, though in a different sense they were mine.

After seven years of marriage and the birth of four children, during most of which time we had a small and neglected plot in which nothing much grew except a vast tree of Bramley apples, we moved to share a large house with my recently widowed mother-in-law. The garden was large, with a huge lawn which had been a tennis court, but soon became a cricket pitch, football ground, space-hopper race-course for the numbers of children who used to drift in and out (we were almost next door to the lovely and apparently free-and-easy Dragon school, where in due course three of our children were pupils). My mother-in-law happily took charge of the rest of the garden, with the help of an ancient gardener who came with the house; and I reverted to childhood, enjoying the garden but taking virtually no responsibility for it. Fifteen years on, with five children, some now undergraduates, we moved again, into central Oxford, where Geoffrey, my husband, had been appointed Principal of Hertford College, just opposite the Bodleian Library. There we lived for 17 years; and there I realised for the first time how hugely important to me the existence of a garden had been. We managed to create a bed in front of the Lodgings and one behind. And we greatly enjoyed planting things there, including what became an enormous magnolia, which now dominates Radcliffe Square when it is in flower. But there was no private garden, nowhere to sit outside with a book (which I still think of as one of the the main purposes of a garden, the proper and desired reward for all the labour), no flowers to pick, and of course no source of fruit and vegetables. People used to try to comfort me by saying 'but you're so close to New College garden, and Wadham, and the University Parks'. But, though I loved all of these, they were not mine. There was no privacy; there were no choices to be made; there was, in short, no ownership. So we soon bought a tiny house, for vacations and weekends, on the edge of Oxfordshire in the village of Great Coxwell. It had been the village schoolmaster's house, and the school behind it had already been converted into a big house. But we had the playground and orchard that had belonged to the school.

We moved in the summer of 1976, the hottest, driest summer anyone could remember, when hosepipes were used to carry washing-up and bath water into the garden, but were otherwise strictly banned. Our first task was to remove the asphalt of the playground and prepare it to be a lawn. Outside the house there was a wide terrace, below that the playground, then two steps down, with a great rockery each side, then a shady orchard going down to a tiny stream. We took turns with the pickaxe, while the other sat on the terrace drinking great quantities of grapefruit juice, sometimes laced with gin. We got top-soil down, and when the rain mercifully came in September, we sowed the grass. We had thoroughly mixed our labour with the lawn, when at last it became a lawn. At Christmas we planted rose hedges round the orchard and on the far side of the stream; but it was the rockery that drove us out of the house in the end (that, combined with the fact that Great Coxwell was not a proper village, as we soon discovered, but a Swindon dormitory). I am very fond of the small things that grow in rockeries, and that can make other people's gardens look good, bright and well-cared for. But the things shrivelled and died in our rockery, and weeds and, above all, grass took over. It seemed that to keep it as anything but an eyesore and source of shame would be a backbreaking full-time job for which neither us had either time or skill. Robin Lane Fox would doubtless have turned it into a glory.

So we moved to a bigger house, this time brand new, indeed not even finished when we bought it, and big enough for us to think happily of retiring to it when the time came. It was built on the side of a steep hill above the village of Axford, near Marlborough in Wiltshire. I had quite wanted to move to somewhere near Winchester, but Geoffrey, having been at school there and having actively hated it, leaving as soon as he was old enough to join the army, had an aversion for Winchester. So we chose the Marlborough Downs instead, with the same chalky soil which I somehow knew in my bones I was destined to battle with. The house had a marvellous view across the Kennet valley to more downs beyond and the edges of Savernake Forest. It was a lovely house and we were proud especially of the enormous L-shaped drawing room and the big kitchen next door to it. It had a steep curving drive, at the bottom of which there was a small fruitful orchard once again dominated by a huge Bramley apple tree, but with room to put in a plum tree and currant bushes. To get from the orchard, if you didn't go up the drive, you climbed a steep flight of steps that brought you onto the big platform cut out of the downs, on which the house was built. There was plenty of room, by our standards, between the steps and the house for a lawn and as many flower beds and vegetable plots as we could manage. The challenge was the banks, between the garden and the fields and downs on one side and the garden and the drive on the other, and between the garden and the orchard, each side of the steps. And when we moved in, the whole garden and the banks were simply snow-white chalk. It was like one of the many great chalk-pits that I remembered from childhood, being always convinced that not I but my beloved Nanny, who looked after us all, and later helped whenever one of our new babies was born, would fall over the edge of one of them and be killed. There were similar chalk-pits round Axford, too, no longer frightening, but full of wild roses and birds in summer, and blackberries in September.

The challenge of this newly exposed plot was to make it capable of growing anything at all except the scabious and other chalk-loving wild flowers that grow on the downs. We could put down topsoil on the flat bit of the garden, as we had over the playground at Coxwell. But to plant the banks with anything meant hacking holes with the faithful pickaxe, and using quantities of compost. In one of the towering banks up to the fields we got a little platform made, with steps up from the lawn and a curved back, like a miniature theatre, much used, as an addition to the wide path all round the house, for my favourite sitting outside, but also by small grandchildren for various kinds of declamation and showing off. Mostly we managed to cover the banks with ground-cover roses, which gradually came to seem my deliciously smelling allies in the fight against nature, and I managed better to turn a blind eye to the grass that grew up among them, better hidden than the grass in the hated rockery. Peonies flourished wonderfully in the beds, and all kinds of dianthus. Our ownership of this flower garden was absolute: it was ours and we made it. There is no doubt that the element of creativity involved in making or planning a garden is what causes it to be the quintessential example of ownership (designing or building a house for oneself would be the same). It is not merely that one takes possession of the land by cultivating it, but that one perpetually makes decisions of detail, like a painter with his canvas or a composer with his score. One's aesthetic judgements and taste are involved, to make the outcome one's own in the most intimate connection, that of an artist with his work.

We were much less successful with vegetables, but here the enemy was not the chalkiness of the soil, so much as the rabbits that came across from the other side of our drive, where there was a huge rabbit warren; and above all the pheasants. There was one particularly pestilential pheasant, named Eric by us after the then Dean of Christ Church in Oxford, to whom he bore a strong resemblance, especially when the Dean was in his finery at Christmas and Easter. The pheasant had the same imperious walk, and look of total disregard for all about him as had the Dean processing up the aisle at the Great Festivals. The bird Eric not only wantonly bit buds off flowers and vegetables, not eating them, but leaving them round the plant to show that he had been there, but he also took to coming into the house, if a French window were left open, and knocking on it if it was shut. Once, when Geoffrey was already ill, Eric crashed through a (luckily empty) bedroom window, and I had to smother him in a blanket and hurl him out of the house, with trails of blood and broken glass everywhere. This was the most bloody of my battles against the natural world.

Soon after Geoffrey died, in 1995, I left Axford, where since retirement we had lived most happily. I was motivated to do so partly because I found gardening on a slope, or precipice, increasingly exhausting, and partly because during a particular spell of snow and ice, I had to leave my car at the bottom of the drive, and struggle, constantly slipping, up the drive on foot, clutching the rose bushes for support (when I got in, I found I had left the chop I had bought in London for my supper in the car, so I had to slither down and struggle up again). Another factor was that some years earlier I had detected Japanese knotweed beginning to grow beside the steps up from the orchard. This was a battle, as I took some time to realise, that I really could not win. I virtuously told the person who bought the house what was going to happen unless he took severe measures, but he, a surgeon by profession, was totally uninterested in the garden, and said that it was no problem. Ten years later I was driving along the road past the orchard and saw that it had entirely disappeared under a sea of knotweed. The surgeon, I was told, had died a year before, but I don't think it was the weed that had killed him. But I had failed again to win the gardener's battle against nature. Today, I would probably have been unable to sell the house, since a would-be purchaser must declare the presence of knotweed when seeking a mortgage.

I love moving house and garden, and I am now in possession of a garden, which, as the last three have been, is thankfully flat. The last and best of my Wiltshire gardens had a view over a huge field that ended in the forest, and faced south west. Here for the first time I got professional help in planning and making the garden, which was, when I arrived, a cross between a small child's play area, and something out of the more abstract parts of the Chelsea Flower Show, all blue decking and blue pebbles scattered here and there, as was the strange fashion in the early years of this century. The young man who helped me, then just starting as a landscape gardener, was kind enough to let me seem to make all the decisions, and his partner, a beginning plantswoman, was equally non-bossy, so I did not at all lose the sense of creativity that belongs to gardening

Although deer were often to be seen in the field beyond, they never came as far as my garden, and there were no rabbits and few pheasants so I grew all the beans and chard that I wanted. And for the last three of my six years in the garden, red kite had begun breeding in the forest and used to come wheeling and playing overhead, sometimes alone, sometimes in groups of ten or twelve. But failing sight rendered me unfit to drive, so I moved to South East London, in the perfect house for living in alone, and with two gardens, one at the back and one, larger, in the front, a curious diamond-shaped plot, characteristic of the vast housing estate, put up after the First World War, of which it is part. Once again I made a lawn (not very successfully) in front, where my predecessor had a huge and hideous garage to house his vintage car. One of my new neighbours took this garage down and conveyed it to his allotment single-handed.

Besides being a vintage car fanatic the previous occupant was a keen and skilful gardener, and though his taste did not entirely coincide with mine, I learned to appreciate, if not to love, even his gladioli, which bring brilliance to the garden in August when everything else is over; and his roses, which, though prolific, were too uniformly pink for my taste. But if I could not create, I could improve: I had more roses as a hedge between the lawn and the road, and clematis against the house, which flourished. There were fruit trees at the back, to which I also added some on the front lawn, an undoubted act of showing off, which I am amazed that so few people practise in London; and I grew vegetables when slugs and snails permitted me. I did not mix so much labour with this plot of land; and it certainly would not be true to say that I made it; but I have never been more conscious of the other aspects of having a garden that make it the very essence of ownership: the pride, for a start; the privacy, the extraordinary quiet, the sense that it was my kingdom and no one could dispossess me, and above all that I had the responsibility of keeping it in good shape, and leaving it better than I found it, which I believe I did. And now, finally, I have taken over another garden, one of my children having gone abroad, leaving me to live in her flat in the same part of London. And as I write, I am half thinking of how I am going to plan the garden, which has recently been mostly devoted to cabbages, the passion of my son-in-law in whose eyes flowers are simply a waste of space.

I shall indulge in no more autobiography; or not much. But I believe that this excursion was necessary, not because there has been anything unusual in my experience (except perhaps the frequency of my moves), but rather the opposite. Most gardeners are more skilled than I, but most also have failures as well as successes, and most are determined to improve what they have got, to make as sure as they can that the next season is better than the last, and that they can take pride in what they achieve, and enjoy it. And this, of course, is the essence of ownership.

The garden is an ancient concept. Certainly the author of the book of Genesis knew of it; and there were famous gardens throughout antiquity, particularly outside Rome. The Emperor Hadrian was especially fond of retreating to his villa and garden, and ended by running the empire sitting there in the garden, or in the domed summer house that he built in it. But gardens, until the sixteenth century, tended to be formal, whether they were large like that at Hadrian's villa, or small like the Elizabethan knot gardens. And of course formal gardens continued to exist, and to change according to fashion. Samuel Pepys, for example, records a conversation he had with his acquaintance, Hugh May, 'a very ingenious man', in July 1666, in which May 'discoursed on the present fashion in gardening – to make them plain'. The Elizabethan tradition of profusion of flowers in 'knotted' beds had been abandoned; and some people regretted this. But the French style of gardening, with broad paths or 'walks' was especially suited to English gardens because of the excellence of both grass and gravel: 'we have the best walks of gravel in the world', May is recorded as saying,

> And then for flowers, they are best seen in little plots by themselves, besides that borders spoil the wideness in any new garden. For fruit, the best way is to span the walls quite circularly one within the other to the south, on purpose for the fruit, and leave the walking garden only for that use.[2]

Mr May would have known what he was talking about; he was deputy surveyor of the King's Works, and at the time working on the King's new garden at Greenwich.

The gardens that I have tried to cultivate, my gardens, have been cottage gardens, unlike the grand gardens about which Hugh May laid down the law. I shall return to grand gardens below, since they form a crucial part of the story of ownership. But first I must say a bit more about the ownership of cottage gardens. For cottage gardens are what most people own, and are that in which they take pride. Farm workers who lived in tied cottages, generally, from feudal times, had a small piece of land that they could cultivate for growing vegetables and they would perhaps keep chickens for their own table. If there were flowers, these filled odd spaces, or, characteristically, climbed up the walls, or over the porch. 'The roses round the door make me love mother more'. So used to sing my Nanny, who grew up in the cottage at the end of the drive to Houghton Lodge in Hampshire where her father was head gardener. By the

---

[2] R.C. Latham and W. Matthews (eds), *The Diary of Samuel Pepys* (Bell & Hyman, London 1972) vol. 7 p. 213.

seventeenth century, however, at the same time as grand gardens were being designed for wealthy owners, with flowers playing a minor role, flower gardens, or 'cottage' gardens with vegetables as well as flowers, were becoming gentrified; indeed, gardening was becoming a passion throughout all classes of society, especially in England. Vegetables and fruit were still grown for their utility, but flowers became increasingly important for purely aesthetic reasons, and many new species of both flowers and trees were introduced from abroad.

There were many reasons for the popularity of gardening. It was partly to do with the English climate, which is peculiarly suited to growing grass. Many gentlemen's houses, standing in modest grounds had outdoor bowling alleys, otherwise lawns. Francis Bacon, writing of gardens, observed 'Nothing is more pleasant than green grass finely shorn'.[3] Keith Thomas, quoting Bacon, remarks that the invention of the lawn-mower in 1830 put this pleasure within the reach of many.[4] In the same chapter, Thomas also attributes the ubiquitous love of gardening, which grew throughout the early modern period, to the peculiarly English love of both property and privacy – both aspects, as I argue, of ownership itself.

There was another kind of gardener, too, who regarded his garden as useful and beautiful, certainly, but also as a place where nature could be treated not as an enemy to be subdued, but as an equal possessor of the garden, to be closely observed and deeply loved. The best known of these is Gilbert White, whose *Natural History and Antiquities of Selborne* was first published in 1789, towards the end of his life, and has never been out of print since. The book takes the form of a series of letters to two fellow naturalists, Thomas Pennant, a professor of zoology, and Daines Barrington, a lawyer, but also a Fellow of the Royal Society. Some of these letters were expanded from a real correspondence, but others were never sent, being written especially for the book. The book itself, rambling and discursive as it is, gives a picture of the whole village, but it arose from the diaries and calendars that White kept of his own garden, with meticulously observed details of the successive seasons each year compared with

---

[3] Francis Bacon, *Essays* (World's Classics, Oxford 1937) p. 190.

[4] Keith Thomas, *Man and the Natural World* (Penguin Books, Harmondsworth 1980) p. 239.

others since the calendars started, and with notes of the appearances and disappearances of all the flora and fauna.

In the eighteenth century, Selborne was an astonishingly hidden village. It was away from the main Roman road running north from Winchester, fifteen or so miles away, and could be approached only down a rutted track. The village lies in a valley with extremely steep, wooded hills on two sides, and behind the village street there is a criss-cross of low tracks, well below the level of the surrounding ground, that have sunk deep into the chalky soil through constant use. These tracks were, and still are, deeply rutted and often impassable because of the mud, or even flowing water. Although access from Petersfield and Winchester has by now been secured, the geographical features of Selborne itself have hardly changed, and it still feels like a closed-in world apart. Gilbert White lived for almost all of his life in a house called Wakes, acquired by his grandfather, who had been Vicar of St Mary's, Selborne, and who bought the house for his wife to live in after he died. There Gilbert's father and mother joined her when he was about nine years old. After studying at Oriel College, Oxford, and taking Holy Orders, and after a brief excursion into academic life, as a fellow of Oriel, Gilbert inherited the house from his father, and lived there with one of his sisters for the rest of his life. He became perpetual curate of St Mary's, but never seriously thought of moving to a proper living. It was at Wakes that all his work was done.

One of the consequences of the isolation of Selborne was its profusion of plants and animals and especially of birds. It was the appearance and departure of these that largely (though by no means exclusively) occupied White's thoughts. He was fascinated by the fact of migration (though some people at this time denied that migration was possible, believing that, for example, swallows hid themselves in barns or even in ponds during the winter). Every first sighting and first song was recorded, and compared on the calendar with other years, as was the weather, and the turning of the trees in autumn. White was a keen hands-on gardener, though he employed one faithful and sympathetic man to help, and a small army of 'weeding women' from the village. He was especially devoted to his melon bed. There was a great fashion for growing melons in the mid-eighteenth century; they seemed romantically exotic and grotesque. They were also exceedingly labour-intensive to grow, needing specially constructed earthen houses with soil enriched by manure, and constant protection against frost, excessive rain or, in summer, excessive drought. Countless words in the diaries are devoted to melons. Here and here alone one can see Gilbert White engaged in a familiar uphill struggle against the ways of nature. For the most part, however, he lived in exceptional harmony with nature.

Gilbert White certainly made structural improvements in the Wakes garden, some of them to make place for his melon grounds. But his philosophy of gardening was probably less aesthetic than vaguely theological. He wanted to know everything about the complexity of the lives of plants, birds (especially their migration), and animals, because, as many of his theological contemporaries held, such knowledge gave to a naturalist an insight into the divine mind, which had fitted living creatures so perfectly to their environment (the 'argument to design' upon which White's older contemporary, David Hume, poured such scorn). It is the sense of the integration of himself with his garden that gives White's Selborne its abiding charm; and because the valley where the village lies is so compact, what is his personal property can in effect be extended to encompass the village as a whole. It belongs to him as a bird's nest belongs to its maker. It is difficult to say whether Selborne more properly belongs to him or he to Selborne. Richard Mabey sums it up when he writes 'Gilbert White could perhaps have written the Natural History in some other village; but it would have to have been his *own*'.[5]

At the same time as Gilbert White was working in and enjoying his garden in Selborne, there was a surge in the fashion for landscape gardening, often referred to under the general term, 'improvement'. This is a subject on which a great deal has been written, not surprisingly, since it is a crucial part of the history of aesthetic taste. It could not have happened except at a time of comparative prosperity, or, perhaps more accurately, a time when the gap between the rich and the poor was widening, and when the rich were particularly anxious to display their wealth and prosperity. The pride of ownership became entangled with the pride of good taste. And, among those who could afford to indulge in 'improvement', aesthetic considerations began to predominate. Jonathan Bate observed: 'If you are a peasant or a sailor your relationship with nature will be bound up

---

[5] Richard Mabey, *Gilbert White: A Biography of the Author of The Natural History of Selborne* (Century Hutchinson, London 1986) p. 13; original italics.

with survival; if you live in the luxury of . . . modernity, your relationship with nature will be aesthetic. It will be bound up with the image and the gaze'.[6]

The first of the great landscape gardeners was William Kent. He started as a painter of boats and barges; but, significantly, he aspired to be a painter in the fine arts sense, and spent ten years as a young man scraping a living in Italy. He apparently had no real talent for painting; indeed, after his death Horace Walpole rated him as 'below mediocrity' as a painter, though brilliant as a landscape gardener.

In Italy, Kent's great talent for design was noticed by Lord Burlington, who brought him back to England to design the interior of Burlington House, and continued as his patron. From interiors, Kent turned to the design of gardens; and it was undoubtedly his study of painting in Italy that influenced his vision; 'All gardening is a landscape painting' he is reported to have said. One of his greatest creations was the gardens at Rousham, in Oxfordshire, where as you walk round the garden a series of prospects open up over the river Cherwell and far beyond, a series of landscapes. At Stowe in Buckinghamshire he transformed what had been a formal garden in the Italian style into a 'natural' garden with views of the garden itself, its great artificial lake and numerous temples and bridges, designed to be seen as different landscapes from different stopping places as you walk round the grounds. There is no doubt that this is painterly work; indeed, Kent had no horticultural knowledge at all. But he worked at Stowe with Launcelot (Capability) Brown as the head gardener, and Brown himself took over the completion of the gardens after Kent's death.

By now landscape gardening was a craze; and Capability Brown was probably the most famous of the landscape gardeners, having, as Kent did not, a thorough knowledge of trees and flowers, though possibly less aesthetic vision. Brown was a great tree-planter. In the seventeenth century, trees had been planted to establish ownership of a park or garden. Keith Thomas[7] quotes John Worlidge, who in 1669 wrote a book for estate-owners called *Systema Agricultura*: 'What can be more pleasant than to have the bounds and limits of your own property preserved and continued from age to age by the

---

[6] Jonathan Bate, *The Song of the Earth* (Picador, London 2009) p. 124.
[7] Op. cit., p. 208.

testimony of such living and growing witnesses?'. Others grew trees to avoid overlooking or being overlooked by property that did not belong to them. But Brown designed gardens in which trees were grown in scattered clumps to draw the eye or break up the view in any part of the grounds. 'Capability' Brown was so designated because, when asked by a garden-owner for a design, his first task was to assess the estate's 'capability of improvement'. And improvement generally meant extensive tree-planting, and the smoothing of contours into a somewhat bland uniformity. Horace Walpole, whose *History of the Modern Taste in Gardening* was published in 1780, though he did not mention Brown by name because he was still alive, greatly approved of his work, and commented on the difference his designs had made not merely to individual properties, but to landscape all over England.

Brown's unofficial successor as most sought-after 'improver' was Humphry Repton, the first to describe himself as a 'landscape gardener'. He was not a hands-on gardener like Brown, but he developed a technique, known as 'Red Books', of drawing plans and painting pictures which he superimposed over maps and pictures of the gardens due for improvement, which meant that he could work much faster, and spread his influence even more widely. In her novel, *Mansfield Park*, published in 1814, Jane Austen describes the visit of the Bertram party from the Park to Sotherton, the place owned by the Rushworths, which they were planning to improve. The universal advice was that they should employ Repton for the work. Aunt Norris, extremely close-fisted herself, but fond of spending other people's money, was especially insistent that Repton should be the consultant, expensive though he was. It was simply assumed that he was the best.

But while the work of Brown and Repton was changing the landscape of England, at the same time those who influenced fashionable taste in painting were laying down that some aspects of that natural landscape were especially suitable to be looked at and enjoyed as though they were in fact pictures. This way of looking at nature had at first no direct connection with gardening, but arose out of the extensive debates on the nature of beauty that occupied essayists and philosophers throughout the eighteenth and early nineteenth centuries, and to which I shall return in chapter 6. Briefly, the beautiful was regular, smooth and predictable, and was in contrast with the sublime which was vast and wild, giving rise to ideas that defied and went beyond any possible descriptive language. It was the Herefordshire landowner, Sir Uvedale Price, who in his *Essay on the Picturesque*, published in 1794, suggested that in between the beautiful and the sublime, and as it were forming a bridge between them, came another aesthetic category, the 'Picturesque'. But he did not invent the term. It had already been made fashionable by William Gilpin in an early essay on the garden at Stowe, which was characterised as possessing 'that peculiar kind of beauty that is agreeable in a picture'. The concept was further developed by him in a work published in 1792, entitled *Essay on Picturesque Beauty*. There he listed the ingredients present in some views of nature, roughness, ruggedness, variety and irregularity that would look well in a picture. Thus at the centre of the meaning of the term is the ambiguous idea of 'landscape', referring either to a genre of representative painting, or to a 'view', what you see before you when, for example, you climb Box Hill, or visit some other beauty spot. The latter aspect of the idea was popularised by Gilpin in his famous *Tours*, published between 1770 and 1789, and consisting of guided tours of the Wye Valley, the Lake District, North Wales and Scotland. Their avowed purpose was 'to examine the face of a country by the rules of picturesque beauty, opening the sources of those pleasures which are derived from the comparison'.

The landscape painter from whom these 'rules' were principally deduced was Claude Lorrain, though there were others who painted in the same style. Lorrain's landscapes often had animals or peasants in the foreground, distant hills in the background, and in the middle ground a decrepit cottage, or a ruin covered in moss or ivy, with tumbling stones suggesting both antiquity and continuity. The importance of the ruin to the picturesque scene was that, according to Gilpin, it showed how a manmade construction, through the effects of time, might become almost a part of nature, or of landscape itself. The variety and apparently random distribution of these objects constituted the 'rule' for the picturesque that Gilpin made into a formula.

The Picturesque became another craze. At its height, people would go out armed with a Claude Lorraine Glass, a convex mirror across which various tinted screens could be drawn and which, if you turned your back on the landscape itself, enabled you to see its reflection in an oval frame, like a Claude picture. The countryside itself was taken over by its image. Jane Austen was working on the first draft of her first novel, *Sense and Sensibility*, in the 1790s, when the fashion for the picturesque was at its height. Although the novel was not published until 1811, she could still incorporate her heroine Marianne's effusions on landscape without need of explanation. Marianne is talking to Edward Ferrars, who is loved by her sister Elinor, on the occasion of his first visit to the family after their move to Somerset. She eagerly questions him about his impressions of the pretty valley where they live. He replies:

> 'You must not inquire too far, Marianne – remember I have no knowledge in the picturesque and I shall offend you by my ignorance and want of taste if we come to particulars. I shall call hills steep which ought to be bold, surfaces strange and uncouth which ought to be irregular and rugged; and distant objects out of sight, which ought only to be indistinct through the soft medium of hazy atmosphere.' 'It's very true' said Marianne 'that admiration of landscape has become a mere jargon. Everybody pretends to feel and tries to describe with the taste and elegance of him who first defined what picturesque beauty was. I detest jargon of every kind and sometimes I have kept my feelings to myself because I could find no language to describe them in but what was worn and hackneyed out of all sense and meaning'. (*Sense and Sensibility* chapter XXVII)

But she looks pityingly at Elinor, who is likely to attach herself to someone incapable of such feeling.

The year after the publication of *Sense and Sensibility*, the caricaturist, Thomas Rowlandson brought out what was his most popular work, *Dr Syntax in Search of the Picturesque*, a series of cartoons accompanied by explanatory verses which pointed out the absurdities inherent in the craze, including a drawing of Dr Syntax making a picturesque landscape out of a signpost, and another of his being surrounded by far from tranquil and harmonious cows. The Picturesque was still worth lampooning well into the nineteenth century.

Before this, however, Uvedale Price, in his 1794 *Essay on the Picturesque*, to which I have already referred, had explicitly brought the concept from the realm of landscape into that of landscape gardening. The essay was an attack on the work of Launcelot Brown, and a plea that the picturesque should be the criterion of improvement in gardens. Instead of the smoothness of perfect classical temples and stretches of artificial water, conspicuous features of the gardens at Stowe, he wanted nature and the garden to flow into one another. And by nature, he meant the beautiful art-inspired nature of the picturesque. The newly invented sunken ha-ha would replace the boundary belts of trees, Greek temples would be replaced by ruins and tumbledown cottages, and smooth walks by rambling paths; there would be cows or sheep on the lawns, and even real hermits in the grottoes. As with all fashions, there was a strong element of snobbishness at work here; Brown, though he became famous and extremely rich, was after all a working gardener. Uvedale Price was a cultivated man who had done the Grand Tour. His family had long owned the estate where he lived, and his uncle was that Daines Barrington who was Dean of Christ Church, Oxford, and the correspondent of Gilbert White. At any rate, Price's *Essay* gave rise to immense controversy, which continued, as we have seen, into the next century.

Eventually as fashions will, the fashion for the Picturesque died, whether on account of the mockery called down on it by its extreme forms, or because gardening was becoming increasingly a suburban and middle-class preoccupation, at odds with aesthetic theorising, a widespread 'hobby' no longer the preserve of the wealthy landowner. At any rate the Victorian love of flowers came to prevail, and more and more women involved themselves in gardening. By the Edwardian age, women could be said to dominate the field, among whom Gertrude Jekyll could claim pre-eminence. Besides designing her own and many other gardens, she wrote not only numerous books but also dozens of gardening articles in magazines, so that her taste was widely disseminated. It was for gardens consisting, like houses, of different 'rooms' each with its own colour, its own style, and its own privacy. In some ways hers, like that of the picturesque gardeners, could be said to be painterly gardening (she had studied art at the Kensington School of Art in the 1860s); but this was because she seemed to think in terms of sweeps of colour across the living canvas. Some attributed this to her love of the Impressionist painters, others to the fact of her poor eyesight, which meant that this was how best she actually saw her gardens. But, whatever the cause, the relationship between actual painting and her gardens, as well as those many gardens inspired, if not designed, by her, was entirely different from that of the picturesque gardeners. As the typical Edwardian garden sprang up, so did innumerable water-colour paintings representing them.

One of Gertrude Jekyll's most successful books was entitled *Some English Gardens*, published in 1904. It is virtually a commentary on thirty watercolour paintings of mostly Italian-inspired English gardens, but includes one of her superb spread of Michaelmas daisies in her own garden at Munstead Wood, near Godalming in Surrey, a house designed, like so many houses in Surrey by Sir Edwin Landseer Lutyens, with whom Gertrude Jekyll closely collaborated over many years. The paintings in this book were by a fellow student at the Kensington Art School, George S. Elgood, who had a lasting passion for Italy.[8] In Elgood's paintings, as in the work of the many, variously talented, watercolourists of the time, art was intended to be the accurate representation of the natural garden (think of all the calendars depicting 'cottage gardens' produced throughout the twentieth century). At the height of the picturesque craze, nature, whether the landscape or the garden, was intended to represent art.

How did this curious reversal come about? In chapter 6 I shall try to throw some light on this by a consideration of the contrast, even conflict, between what is owned and what is not, which lies at the heart of the romantic view of nature. But before this I must examine some different aspects of ownership, for so far we have been concerned only with the individual's ownership of property, essentially of that which is mine and not yours, and over which I exercise unique rights and responsibilities. But ownership may also be common; and it would be impossible to conduct a full investigation of the notion without at least a selective enquiry into what it is to own a thing in common, and whether this kind of ownership has its own distinctive 'feel'.

---

[8] *Some English Gardens* was republished under the title *Classic English Gardens* with an introduction by Sally Festing (Studio Editions, London 1995).

4. Common ownership 1: communism

> Private property is a necessary institution, at least in a fallen world. Men work more and dispute less when goods are private than when they are common. But it is to be tolerated as a concession to human frailty, not applauded as a good in itself.

So wrote the pioneering social theorist and economist, R.H. Tawney.[1] Unlike Hume, he did not think that the ownership of property was anything to be proud of. But immediately we come across an ambiguity. Although in the passage quoted he spoke of common, as the alternative to private, ownership (and was writing in the context of the early Christian ideal of holding all things in common), in fact he was a socialist through and through, and the real alternative to private ownership that he advocated was state ownership, of land, of houses, and especially of schools. We shall see, in the course of this chapter, how slippery a notion common ownership becomes when set up as an ideal; how it slides between the idea, on the one hand, of people sharing ownership among themselves and, on the other hand, that of the state owning things in the name of the people who are its citizens. In order to be able to think of state ownership as a species of common ownership, one has repeatedly to remind oneself that in a democracy the people are sovereign, or that, as Locke held, in the last resort, government can act only with the continuing consent of the people. State ownership could, in theory, be dismantled at a stroke by overthrowing the state, or the sovereign government of that state. But unless there were some other sovereign to give the law its authority, no property would be secure; the concept of legitimate ownership of any kind would disintegrate, and a Hobbesean 'state of nature' would ensue. Property, as opposed to mere possession, as

---

1 R.H. Tawney, *Religion and the Rise of Capitalism* (Harcourt, Brace & World, New York 1926).

we have seen, depends on the rule of law, whether that property is public or private. However, such highly abstract speculation gives us little clue to the reality of common ownership, in whatever its form, which is to be the subject of this chapter and the next, and to which we must now turn.

First, we must consider the matter historically. After the French Revolution, and the overthrow of the ancient regime, political thought was for decades preoccupied with the relation between owners and non-owners, between the rich and the poor, the haves and have-nots, ownership of money being as important as ownership of land. This issue replaced the question that had preoccupied Locke and his contemporaries, of the legitimacy of political power, or rather it transformed the question. For of course with wealth went power, and in France the populist aim had been to strip the aristocracy and the church of both wealth and power in one blow. The hope was that the revolution would result in a radical redistribution of both power and property.

However, throughout this chapter, in which we shall consider the various kinds of socialism, mutualism and communism, advocacy of which followed the French Revolution, and which culminated in the communism of Marx and Engels, we shall find a certain vagueness and equivocation in the idea of the ownership of property. There is a distinction, important to the law of inheritance, between private and personal property. Private property, by and large, is thought of as land and those immovable objects, such as buildings, that occupy land. Personal property, or chattels, consists of movable things such as livestock, furniture, clothes and jewellery. If we lived in a primitive society, this dichotomy would embrace everything that could be owned; and if it were part of the law of that society that one might pass on one's land to one's children, or indeed that one's land must pass to one's eldest son, then the distinction between private and personal property would become very important. In such a society one could imagine a father accumulating personal property which he could then will to his other children, if he so wished, or the children might hold the chattels in common, and doubtless dispute over them, as Tawney would have foreseen. But this is mere mythology. What in reality changed everything, as Locke knew, was the existence of money. Someone's wealth can consist of nothing but money; and someone's chattels can be exchanged for money. I may own a racehorse, or the Eustace diamonds, as readers of Anthony Trollope will know, and my legatees may be exceedingly anxious to get their hands on them for the reason that they are worth money.

But the other great change, no less radical, was the development of the technology that made it possible for the first time to cultivate land for commercial purposes, then, still more important, to manufacture goods on a large scale. Land was no longer the sole source of produce, nor artisan-made tools the sole means of production. The revolutionaries bent on overthrowing the aristocracy and the Church were in a way barking up the wrong tree. They perhaps did not, in the heat and excitement of 1789, fully realise that they were triumphing over an enemy who was half way to being beaten already, by the owners, not of land, but of money and the new source of money, manufacturing industry (we have to remember that the Industrial Revolution hit France very late, in comparison with England). The confusion between different kinds of ownership that we noticed in Tawney is reflected in the differing aims of the revolutionaries and their successors in France. Sometimes when socialism calls for the abolition of private property what is meant is the ownership of land; sometimes what is meant is the ownership of manufacturing companies and services such as banks and canals. Sometimes what is meant may even include the ownership of personal property. We have to bear this equivocation in mind throughout what follows; for, as we shall see, it compounds the confusion and vagueness that shrouds the envisaged future for all post-revolutionaries: how are we going to live when the revolution is over? What will it actually be like?

However, before pursuing what is to be the main subject of this chapter, I must first turn to the towering figure of Jean-Jacques Rousseau (he will appear again when we come to consider the consequences of the romantic concept of nature, in chapter 6). At school I was taught history as a series of causes and effects. We each had a notebook divided into columns, in which we entered Events, Dates, Causes, Consequences. Alongside the event of the Fall of the Bastille, beside the date, was to be entered as cause 'the publication of Rousseau's *Social Contract*'. I suppose that this judgement was derived largely from my history teacher's devotion to Thomas Carlyle; but it had a persisting effect on my ability to understand Rousseau when, as an undergraduate, I came to read him. For I could not reconcile what I had been taught as dogma, and which, as such things do, still reverberated in my brain, with what I then read, an author averse to violence, whose work seemed to have little relevance to nation-states. It seemed capable of application, if anywhere, only in small communities, such as the Swiss Cantons with which Rousseau was acquainted, or ancient Sparta, the Greek city-state he most admired, where the whole people could meet together, and thrash out what was truly the common good, expressed in the general will.

It is tempting to suppose that it was the great rhetoric of the first sentence of the *Social Contract*, 'Man is born free but everywhere is in chains' that gave the work such potency as it had. But Rousseau goes on to state that, though he does not know how this phenomenon came about, 'what can make it legitimate, that I think I can say'. So from the start, the book is not a rallying cry to escape from bondage, but a guide to what kind of state will allow that bondage to be perfect freedom. For if men make their own laws, they have chosen how to live, and they are therefore free, though bound to obedience. It is a Kantian thought. Men are free if and only if they legislate for themselves. The people exercise their free will in binding themselves to obey. This is what Rousseau designates the 'General Will', which will lead to the common good.

The idea of the general will remains, to me at least, mysterious. For, by definition, the general will is supposed to be that which is directed towards the common good. And Rousseau's great problem was to give an intelligible account of how this common good was to be discovered. A majority vote in an assembly of everyone would not necessarily lead to its discovery, since men would most probably be biased towards their own interests; and if they grouped together into parties or factions, this would be even more divisive and disastrous as far as concerned any agreement as to what constituted the common good. They would be in danger of losing sight of any common goal, in the interest of party. In the end his solution seems to rest on the belief that there would always spontaneously emerge a figure, to whom he refers as the 'Legislator', who would know what was the common good, and, by his charisma and natural authority, would produce a consensus. Men would thus, in Rousseau's somewhat sinister words, be 'forced to be free', that is, to cast their vote on the side of whatever the Legislator proposed as the common good.

However, though Rousseau's work may not have had the causal responsibility for the French Revolution ascribed to it by Carlyle and my history teacher, he may nevertheless be seen as engaged in setting out what would be the ideal political constitution, and thus as the first of the utopia-writers who flourished after the revolution was over, some of whom we shall now consider.

Many of these visionary thinkers and political theorists were assembled in Paris in the early decades of the nineteenth century. It was a time of turmoil all over Europe, and a number of radical thinkers, as well as artists and musicians, escaped the hostility of their own countries, or indeed were thrown out of them, to the extraordinarily open-minded and intellectually lively atmosphere of Paris. Political confusion and constant changes of government stimulated rather than inhibited conversations, salons, the exchange of ideas. It was here that the utopia-writers were mainly assembled.

The first of them was the highly aristocratic Claude Henri de Rouvroy, Comte de Saint-Simon. Saint-Simon was in some respects an heroic figure, identifying himself with the interests of those who had overthrown his inherited ascendancy. He was the first writer to perceive the revolution as a clash between classes to be defined in economic terms, as those who owned and those who did not own property. But he also understood that it was largely science and technology that would determine the future. He therefore envisaged an ideal society in which the educated class, scientists, inventors, entrepreneurs, bankers, should hold political power, since it was they, not the manual workers, who would be able to resist the corrupting effects of power, and use their position for the general improvement of society. In such a society people would be paid properly for what they did, and the injustice that had led to the revolution would disappear. The great change, however, would be the abolition of inheritance. Society would be, and would remain, meritocratic. Saint-Simon had a great many followers, many of them, like him, practical and enterprising men. It was Saint-Simonians who got together the money and labour to construct the Suez Canal; Saint-Simon himself spent time designing an ambitious canal-system for Spain, and Saint Simonians were effective in developing the French railway system.

One of the disciples of Saint-Simon was François Marie Charles Fourier. He was a very different person from Saint-Simon, a commercial traveller by trade, the son of a blacksmith, and he lived in Paris for the first decades of the nineteenth century. He did not share Saint-Simon's optimism about the possibility of finding a class of rulers who would be able to resist the corruption that comes from power. Indeed, he saw with his own eyes the bankers and entrepreneurs in the capital making themselves rich, and antagonising, not only the workers, but also the small businesspeople and artisans, the class from which he himself sprang, who could not compete with the mass production now possible in the new factories. He foresaw a time when overproduction by these factories would lead industrialists into competition with one another, to produce goods more and more cheaply, thus forcing down wages so that the poor would starve, not on account of there being too few, but too many goods. In his Utopia, therefore, there would be no central state, nor central government, but numerous small communities, which he named '*Phalanstères*' (phalansteries). Although each would be independent and self-governing there would be some sort of loose federation of them all. For example, there would be one enormous electricity plant that would generate power for all the phalansteries (he was vague about how this was to work, except in so far as he said that all natural resources, including water, were to be held in common between the groups).

Within each of the small groups there would likewise be no private property, everything being held in common. People would be contented, because there would be such division of labour that nobody would do a job uncongenial to him, but everyone could do what he was best at and enjoyed. If someone had to do an uncongenial job, he would be paid extra (though most of the nastiest work would be allocated to Jews, who were regarded by Fourier as devoted entirely to accumulating property and lending money, and therefore were in his view uniquely wicked, and outside the cosy collectivism of the phalansteries).

That this envisaged state of affairs was not even intended to be realistic is shown by the fact that Fourier foresaw a time, quite soon, when new species of animals would evolve, akin to the bears, tigers and squirrels that we now know, but cleverer and less hostile to man. These creatures, 'anti-bears' and 'anti-squirrels', would do much of the manual work that men (and women) have to do in the world in its present stage of evolution, and would thus leave human beings with plenty of time to pursue the things they were uniquely good at, the sciences and the arts.

In spite of his lapses into science fiction, Fourier's vision had much in common with that of Rousseau, who, as we have seen, equally thought that the ideal state should be as small as an ancient city-state. Moreover, they both regarded the process of civilisation as a process of degeneration, a spoiling of the naturally good; and both were deeply concerned, therefore, with how children should be educated, becoming civilised without losing that about them which was naturally unspoiled. Fourier, however, unlike Rousseau, thought that women should have the same rights as men. The great difference between them, however, was that Rousseau was concerned only with the distribution of political power, whereas Fourier, following Saint-Simon and in the light of post-revolutionary experience, saw the question to be one of ownership, or the distribution of wealth. At any rate Fourier was an influential figure, in that numerous phalansteries were formed, especially in America, several of which survived for a considerable time. And the idea of a commune, self-supporting and egalitarian, holding all things in common, is one that is perpetually renewed, short-lived though many such communes are.

The utopia-writer most explicitly concerned with the idea of ownership, and therefore the most relevant to our enquiry was Pierre-Joseph Proudhon. As a young man he was apprenticed to a printer, and in the course of his work was involved in the production of a book by Fourier, published in 1829, entitled *The New Industrial and Societal Order*. This work so much excited him that he gave up his plans to become a printer himself, and instead became, briefly, a member of parliament, and devoted himself to political theory. His name was made by his first book, published in 1840, entitled *What is Property? Or, an Enquiry into the Principle of Right and of Government*. The central argument of his book starts from the axiom that property is the right of increase by the proprietor over anything which he has stamped as his own. But proprietors treat the right to increase a thing or things as the right to production without any contribution of labour on their own part. In Proudhon's view there can be no such right. Like Locke, he held that entitlement to property comes uniquely from the labour that goes into its production. Therefore one must say either that the idea of property as that which is owned without the involvement of labour is contradictory, or that property as currently understood is identical with theft, the holding of goods that do not by right belong to one. Proudhon notoriously chose the latter option: 'property is theft'. Of course, there is a good sense, as we have seen, in which without property there would be no such thing as theft; but such pedantry must not be allowed to spoil the splendid rhetoric of the words. Proudhon was indeed a master of such sound-bites. 'If property can exist only as a right', he says, 'then property is impossible'. And again, 'Under the rule of property, the flowers of industry are woven into none but funeral wreaths. The labourer digs his own grave'. But of course it was not simply that the workers were being deprived of what, by their labour, was rightly theirs; but that the bankers and industrialists upon whom Saint-Simon had relied to make a fairer society were seizing not only wealth but also political power, and gradually destroying the classes that were under their domination.

It is doubtful whether Proudhon would have read Hegel, but a vague and misty Hegelianism was undoubtedly in the atmosphere in Paris at this time, the ideas coming in with the many German emigrés who were arriving in the city. Everyone would know that history proceeds by the inevitable clash of one force against another, the thesis, the antithesis, and then the synthesis, in which Spirit would ultimately triumph. So Proudhon argued that competition was the great evil, setting one class against another, and that this evil could be overcome only by a different system called 'Mutualism', in which it was acknowledged that one class needs the other, that if cooperation replaced capitalism, if private property was limited, though not eliminated, the extremes of greed, leading to the accumulation of wealth, and deprivation would come to an end. It was to be a regime of moderation. Cooperative banks (not unlike those proposed by Justin Welby, Archbishop of Canterbury, in 2013) would lend money, but at affordable interest rates, so that gradually the poor would be able to better themselves, and a sense of justice would prevail.

These were some of the ideas eagerly discussed and even to some extent tried out in Paris in the first part of the new century (Proudhon himself joined a mutualist group in Lyons, and later transferred it, or set up its equivalent, in Paris). This was the Paris that Karl Marx (1818–1883) entered for the first time in 1843. He came as a fully paid-up Hegelian, having learned the theory of historical inevitability at the University of Berlin. After graduating, for a time he ran a newspaper in Cologne, but was expelled for his radical opinions and, like many of his countrymen, went to the intellectually liberal haven of Paris. He had read and admired Proudhon's *What is Property?*; the courageousness of the opinions and the racy style appealed to him, and he probably met and talked with Proudhon soon after his arrival. However, Proudhon sent him a copy of his next book, whose subtitle was *The Philosophy of Poverty*, and Marx was disgusted by it. He responded by publishing a withering reply in a pamphlet called *The Poverty of Philosophy*, in which he inveighed against the moralistic tone of Proudhon's book. It expressed nothing but his preferences, he wrote, and he reduced the coming conflict to a kind of battle of good against evil, as if one could pick and choose, eliminating the evil and leaving the good intact. Proudhon's book, *The System of Economic Contradiction*, or *The Philosophy of Poverty*, appeared in 1846; and by this time Marx, though still, and always, owing a great debt to Georg W.F. Hegel as far as the pattern of historical development was concerned, had in fact left Hegel behind.

Hegel (and all the Parisian utopia-writers) believed that ideas shaped history. The idea of feudalism, the idea of property and power, the idea of socialism all brought about the material condition of societies. Marx, on the other hand, had come to believe that it was the other way round. It was the economic conditions in which different classes in society lived, their material environment, that gave birth to the ideas. Marx had come to despise the Hegelian concept of the 'spirit of the age', a set of ideas and assumptions which determined the economic circumstances of the age, and which could itself emerge as a new spirit, when the inevitable conflict was over. Even more, he despised the socialist notion that if the working class could wrest power from the aristocracy, justice would be restored, and a new cooperative harmony between the previously conflicting classes would remain. Such moral absolutes as justice and harmony had become anathema to him. As he said, they expressed what those who embraced them would like to see, and had nothing to do with the way, as a matter of scientific fact, the history of human society, throughout the world, was going to develop. According to Marx, in the natural world, the world that constitutes the subject matter of the natural sciences, what distinguishes men from other animals is not their self-consciousness or their reason, but the fact that they and they alone produce what they need for subsistence. Thus society is developed from this fact of production, which is the dynamic of history, and indeed the only reality that there is. Writing in 1845, and referring to Hegelian historians, Marx wrote:

> [This history] takes account . . . only of the political, literary and theological aspects of the principal historical events. Just as it separates thought from sense experience, mind from body, itself from the world,

> so it separates history from natural science and industry, and sees the birthplace of history, not in vulgar material production on earth, but in the cloudy regions of heaven.[2]

It is impossible to exaggerate the difference that his materialism makes to Marx's view of historical inevitability and the outcome of revolution, or how far it separates him from the Parisian socialist utopia-writers we have been considering.

While he was still in Paris, before being yet again exiled, and taking up residence in England (the only country that would have him, though it hardly took him to its heart), Marx had the good fortune to meet Friedrich Engels, who became his indispensable partner. Engels had made a study of the condition of factory workers in Manchester, and was therefore able to supply Marx with the facts on which his theory of capital had to be based. They worked closely together for the rest of Marx's life; indeed most of Marx's written output was as much Engels's work as his own. The exception is *The Communist Manifesto*, a first draft of which Engels produced as a set of questions and answers, which Marx abandoned, to produce instead one of the most direct and stirring political documents ever written, for presentation to the newly formed International, in 1848.

The International was formed, with Marx for a considerable time at its head, as a result of a delegation of German workers who came over to England and met with their English counterparts. Marx had become certain (and he never doubted this thereafter) that communism must be an international movement or nothing; the proletariat was not a class standing in opposition to class enemies in particular states, whose actions would be determined by the particular circumstances obtaining in those states, but existed as one unified historical phenomenon, poised eventually not to overcome the capitalists and replace them, but to bring the class system, owners of property and their virtual slaves, entirely to an end. The state, which existed only as a means to maintain the balance between the inevitably conflicting interests of the classes, would itself become unnecessary, would indeed 'wither away'. The names of states, Germany, France and the rest, would indicate not a political structure, but simply a geographical space where people lived and spoke for the most part the same

[2] 'Die Heilige Familie' in Marx–Engels *Gesamtausgabe* vol. 1 sec. 3 p. 137.

language, ordering their own affairs through the production and distribution of material goods.

Marx did not, of course, deny the existence of ideas. How could he, as he struggled to produce the economic ideas of *Das Kapital*? And he admired the French, writing that there was a political theorist in every Frenchman, this in contrast with the Germans who were too stupid to think in general terms. It was rather that, just as a materialist holds at the level of the individual that what one thinks is the expression of the changes that occur in one's body, especially one's brain, so at the level of groups, it is their material conditions that are expressed in their theories and their actions. There is no separate 'spirit'; and no separate 'will'.

But the trouble with any theory of historical inevitability, whether the inevitable conflicts and resolutions are derived from ideas or from material conditions, is that it may lead to inertia. Material conditions form a set of given facts which are as they are; but they are destined to change. Why should the workers not wait? Why should they try to exercise a fictitious determining will of their own, thereby, incidentally, turning Marx's theory on its head, and supposing that ideas of the future can bring that future about? Yet Marx, with the help of Engels, was driven to urge the workers to action, to encourage them to be on the side of history and join its movement, to envisage the future of the classless society unhampered by private ownership.

This could be done only by inducing in the workers a sense of solidarity with others all over Europe, which would itself generate a motive and a sense of the possibility of success. The task was even harder than it might have been, given the context of numerous failed and partial uprisings in Europe, none of which came, in outcome, anywhere near the vision (based as he thought on scientific fact) to which Marx was committed. It was no wonder that the emphasis came to be more and more on the inevitability of the ultimate outcome, world communism and the end of private ownership, rather than on the details of what it would be like when it came. Marx had little to say about the problems that had preoccupied the utopia-writers, namely how to prevent the corruption of those who would take power after the revolution. For him it was enough that there would be no more classes, and therefore no parties between whom conflict could arise.

In fact there was no communist revolution until long after

Marx's death. The Russian revolution of 1917 did not, of course, come out of the blue. As early as 1905, on Bloody Sunday, hundreds of unarmed people, protesting against their poverty and powerlessness, had been shot down by imperial troops. Nicolas II was a conspicuously tyrannical Czar, who believed not only in the divine right of the Romanovs to rule, but also in his own unique knowledge of what was right for the Russian people, whose loyalty and love he believed that he commanded. The war with Germany which broke out in 1914 brought immense suffering not only to the army, but also to people as a whole, with acute shortages of food; and it substantially increased the already great unpopularity of Nicholas's wife, Alexandra, who was German. The revolution, when it started, was an outbreak of excitement and popular feeling; Nicholas II was forced to abdicate and a provisional government was established, which lasted, however, only a few months. By this time the Bolsheviks were the dominant revolutionary party, led by Vladimir Lenin. He was a Marxist, and had been exiled for his radical theories, and especially for those contained in his book *What Is to Be Done?*. In this he argued that future revolutions should be conducted by professional soldiers, rather than by a disorderly rabble of untrained enthusiasts. And this is what in fact happened during the civil war which followed the 1917 outbreak. The so-called Red Army confronted the White imperial army and defeated them. Meanwhile government, consisting of representatives from the soviets, or workers' groups, was concentrated in the Kremlin, and was a one-party dictatorship from the first. Farms became collectively owned; and this was very much what the peasant classes had wanted. But as far as industry went, Lenin was more concerned with the electrification of all plants and the improvement of transport than with public, let alone worker, ownership. It was not until after his death that private ownership of industry and retail business was absolutely abolished, the press controlled and criticism of the government in any form forbidden. Meanwhile, industrialisation increased at an enormous rate, as well as scientific research and development. Communist Russia as a great power in a remarkably short time became a reality.

But we must ask whether this was indeed a communist country, in any sense that would have satisfied Marx. It was certainly socialist, in so far as the state eventually owned industries and public services, as well as agriculture. But 'the State' was a self-perpetuating institution with no kind of accountability to anything but itself. And, though democracy was never any serious part of communism, the Soviet Union could hardly be said to have been a classless society either. For though the majority of people owned very little, not even the flats they lived in, not even a car, the minority, those in government and a favoured few academics, members of the KGB, and government-sponsored scientists, musicians and artists owned a great deal, including houses in town and dachas in the country. Like Marx, neither Lenin nor Joseph Stalin who succeeded him cared for such moral concepts as justice, Stalin's 'purges' and mock trials being particularly odious to those who retained their moral sense. It is therefore extremely difficult now to see how post-revolutionary Russia could have been thought to be the goal to which history was inevitably proceeding; nor even the penultimate goal, the period of socialism that was supposed to lead to the withering away of the state. No state could seem more firmly entrenched.

In a final attempt to discover whether the abolition of private ownership worldwide, which is, after all, the essence of communism, can throw any light on the difference it makes whether you own something or do not, I shall look at some of those Europeans who became enamoured of communism in the 1930s. What was it about communism that so much attracted them? What, in particular, were the hopes of the British Communist Party? The British Communist Party still exists, though in a fairly vestigial form. I have talked to one of its loyal members, but his conversation, though learned and amusing, was about the distant past. He was steeped in the works of Marx, admiring both his economics and his theory of history. He rightly dwelt on the enormous influence Marx had, and still has, on the writing of history; he was a socialist, opposed to the privatisation of previously public industries and services. His passion, however, was for equality, and he was outraged by the emergence of a British 'underclass'. And in this I could entirely agree with him. But he had little to say about the idea of ownership itself. So, rather than relying on one conversation, I shall look briefly at some essays that form a volume published in 1950, in which some of those who had been communists and had given it up, examine their one-time hopes, and how they were disappointed.[3]

---

[3] Richard Crossman (ed.), *The God That Failed* (Hamish Hamilton, London 1950).

The first essay, and the one perhaps most directly relevant to the question of ownership, is by the author Arthur Koestler, one of the most influential left-wing writers of the twentieth century. He speaks of his conversion to communism as an act of faith, and, like all such acts, it arose out of deep personal experience, and the hope of all utopia-writers, that the future will somehow reproduce the simplicities and the integrity of a mythological past, of which the present is a corruption. He wrote: 'Devotion to the pure Utopia and revolt against a polluted society are the two poles which provide the tension of all militant creeds'.[4] He was, he said, ripe for conversion: his middle-class family (he was born in Bulgaria and educated in Austria) was being squeezed out of existence, ruined by the inflation of the 1920s. Some of the middle classes, he said, turned to the right, becoming Nazis and blaming their fate on Versailles and the Jews. Others turned to the left:

> Thus confirming the prophecy of the Communist Manifesto: 'Entire sections of the ruling classes are . . . precipitated into the proletariat, or are at least threatened in their conditions of existence. They . . . supply the proletariat with fresh elements of enlightenment and progress.' That 'fresh element of enlightenment', I discovered to my delight, was I.[5]

What excited Koestler about the new future was the predicted disappearance of the concept of the family, as much as anything: 'The demonstration of the historical relativity of institutions and ideals – of family, property, class, patriotism, bourgeois morality, sexual taboos – had the intoxicating effect of a sudden liberation from the rusty chains with which a pre-1914 childhood had cluttered one's mind'. And he speaks of the 'emotional fervour and intellectual bliss' which, by 1950, had become difficult to recapture 'when Marxist philosophy has degenerated into a Byzantine cult, and virtually every tenet of the Marxist programme has become twisted into its opposite'.[6]

The last essay in the book is by the poet and critic, Stephen Spender. He was a member of the British Communist Party for only a few weeks, and he describes his initial interview with Harry Pollitt, the long-serving Secretary of the Trades Union arm of the British

4 Ibid., p. 25.
5 Ibid., p. 29.
6 Ibid., p. 30.

Communist Party, and a fierce champion of Stalin's Soviet Union. Pollitt had summoned him after reading his early book *Forward from Liberalism*, in which Spender had argued that the idea of individual freedom with which Liberalism was chiefly concerned must be taken over in future by employees rather than employers (whatever this may mean). Pollitt persuaded him to join the Party, but pointed out that his arguments were all entirely intellectual, not passionate; and that, in particular, a true communist must feel hatred towards capitalism, of which Spender showed no symptom, being a man temperamentally horrified by violence of any kind, and, unlike Koestler, very much rooted in his prosperous and cultivated family.

Spender makes it clear in his autobiographical essay the extent to which, for his generation, communism was seen as a plausible and effective alternative (indeed perhaps the only plausible and effective alternative) to Fascism. It was seen, that is, as essentially a form of government, the transfer of power to the people being central to it, not merely consequential on the transfer of property. He spent some time in Spain as a journalist, during the civil war, and many of his like-minded friends actually volunteered to fight on the anti-Fascist side that was supported by the Russians. The failure of the civil war in Spain was compounded by the feebleness and blindness of the governing classes in Britain, who refused to see Fascism as a threat; and these factors together made enthusiasm for the USSR a natural attitude among intellectuals in Britain. True communists, as Spender points out, were blind to the ruthless methods needed to attain the goal of the revolution, and what would follow it. Moreover, true communists had a mystical faith in the workers. If once they threw off their oppressors the workers would emerge as properly human, an example and type of what humanity really is. Yet Spender was full of rather endearingly snobbish doubts. Did he really want to join the proletariat? As he began to admit to himself, what he wanted was not to become one of the workers, but rather that the workers should become like him, enjoying as he did the privilege of freedom to entertain and explore ideas, not bound by any orthodoxy, not obliged to suppress the truth as he saw it, even if it should fail to coincide with the party line. It was all very well to think that Russia represented a temporary phase of socialism and the dictatorship of the Party, before the Party and the state would wither away. It showed no sign of doing so, and the atrocities committed in the name of communism seemed to increase rather than diminish. Moreover, those of the middle classes who had, in Koestler's words, joined the proletariat seem to have done nothing towards civilising the tastes and preferences of the workers. Any work of art or literature, and any piece of music must appeal instantly to the workers, and above all must cheer them up, in case they should begin to doubt the glorious effects of the revolution. So communism had to be given up, by those, like Spender, who were compassionate in the face of manifest human suffering, and who valued above all things freedom of expression and the pursuit of truth.

Although Marx insisted that communism meant the end of private property, and that by owning the means of production, the proletariat would eventually own that which gave human beings their unique character, yet neither he nor his successors could tell us much about what this ownership would entail, what it would actually be like when it eventually came about, what rights it would confer and on whom. Indeed, though communists had their eyes fixed on the future, regarding any means as justified by the nature of the end towards which history was moving, yet they seemed in some ways completely incurious about what that future would hold, especially for the workers when they came home from the factories that they would now own in common.

Marx himself, however, did throw some glimmer of light on that domestic aspect of ownership. He insisted that human nature is essentially social, and that man is fulfilled only within a social context. But a new social context will replace the traditional family. In *Das Kapital* he suggests that the capitalist exploitation of women and children in the factories will actually work towards the abolition of old-style families: 'Large-scale industry, by assigning, as it does, an important part in the process of production, outside the domestic sphere, to women, to young persons, to children of both sexes, provides an economic basis for a higher form of the family and the relations between the sexes'. The 'Teutonic/Christian' form of the family is only one in a series of forms that have existed in history; and the recognition of this was one of the aspects of communism that so much attracted the young Koestler.

> It is obvious that the effect of the effective working group being composed of both sexes and all ages must necessarily under suitable conditions become a source of humane development; although in its spontaneously developed brutal capitalist form, where the labourer exists for the process

> of production and not the process of production for the labourer, it is a pestilential source of corruption and slavery.[7]

Later, he argues that there will come a time when human beings may relax their ceaseless struggle to produce what is necessary to satisfy their ever-increasing needs, and be free to turn their attention to 'that development of human potentiality for its own sake which is the true realm of freedom'. This, however, 'can flourish only upon the role of necessity as its basis. The shortening of the working day is its prerequisite'.[8] So after the revolution, the proletariat will eventually be able to look forward to a little more leisure within whatever new form of the family will have evolved. And that will be its own reward. But we still do not know how he will use that leisure, except that presumably it will not be to cultivate his garden.

As a footnote, and to round off this consideration of the ownership of the means of production, it is worth noticing how this concept became part of the Labour Party's ideology from its beginning. The first Manifesto, which was drafted by Sidney Webb with the help of George Bernard Shaw, and presented to the party conference of 1918, contained the notorious Clause IV, which became a millstone round the neck of the increasingly middle-class Party of the late twentieth century. This clause promised:

> To secure for workers by hand and by brain the full fruits of their industry and the most equitable distribution thereof that may be possible, on the basis of common ownership of the means of production and broad-based, distribution and exchange; and the best obtainable system of popular administration and control of each industry or service.

As time went on, this clause was seen by both Old Labour and New to run exactly counter not only to the growth of the managerial class, distinct from both owners and workers in all major industries and service-providers, but also to the increasing use of privatisation, and public/private partnerships. Eventually, at the end of the party conference of 1994, just after he had succeeded John Smith as leader of the party, Tony Blair, in a scarcely noticed revolutionary act, announced that he was going to replace Clause IV. Early the following year, at a specially convened conference, the clause was replaced

7 *Das Kapital* I VA I pp. 514–16.
8 Ibid., III VA III/2 pp. 873–4.

by a totally bland and vacuous clause, identifying Labour as a Social Democratic party, and, like a school prospectus, mentioning everyone's fulfilling his potential and living with his fellow citizens in harmony and with respect. Thus any connection with communist ideology or with ownership itself was officially severed. Marx would especially have despised the moralistic language of harmony and respect.

5. Common ownership 2: some more modest forms

Common ownership has frequently been discussed, and indeed practised, in contexts narrower than the global revolutions that Marx had envisaged. For Marx had a general theory of human nature, namely that what distinguishes man from other animals is that he alone produces what will meet his needs, while all other animals rely on finding it. And this theory requires that all the producers of goods, the workers, should regard themselves, worldwide, as one society, owning together both the means of production and what is produced. If such a change in perspective were to be achieved, the relationship between one human being and another would be radically changed, and the whole existing structure of political power thrown into the melting pot.

We have seen that the post-revolutionary Paris utopia-writers did not have anything so radical in their sights when they thought of the possible future. Some of them had followers who set up small communes, especially in the USA, within which everything was held in common for the benefit of all. Many of these had a specifically religious basis, and sought to avoid the supposed corruption of man's sense of duty towards God, nature and fellow human beings by returning to a primitive way of life, everyone, man, woman and child, contributing to the life of the self-supporting, essentially agricultural, community, as little reliant on modern technology as possible, and owning no personal property. Some such austere communities still exist, especially in southern parts of the USA, and are self-perpetuating in so far as children are born for the most part to interrelated members of like communities in the same region. They are a matter of mild and occasional curiosity to the rest of the world, but have no political influence whatsoever.

The 1970s and early 1980s saw a proliferation of such communes, some centred round the religious, or quasi-religious teachings of particular gurus from the Far East, and a source of deep anxiety to many parents of young people in pursuit of the hippy life-style, and, like Marxists before them, liberation from the restrictions of the conventional bourgeois family. Many of these communes collapsed in scandal, drug-related, sexual or financial.[1]

The early Christians were also a model for some later communities. For they were known to have advocated the sharing of all their worldly possessions with one another and with the poor. But most were short-lived, the standards of self-denial, and the lack of privacy involved in the abandonment of ownership, being perhaps too demanding, except for those so dedicated as to take their vows as monks or nuns.

The most long-lasting attempts at communal living, common ownership and shared ideals, yet still short of global or international ambition as a condition of success, have been the Kibbutzim in Israel. The first Kibbutz was set up in 1909 close to the Sea of Galilee. Throughout the early history of the Kibbutz movement there was a strong element of Zionism, as well as a desire to live naturally and self-sufficiently. The idea of collectivity was necessary to their establishment. No individual could afford the capital expenditure involved in setting up the largely agricultural communities, in buying equipment and farming it successfully. Collectively, each could provide part of the capital, and much was supplied by charitable donations from Jews at large. But though communal ownership was a necessity, not a separate and distinct ideal, it was taken very literally and seriously by the kibbutzniks, as a condition of the equality which they regarded as a right for all human beings. Indeed for them (and in this their philosophy was very different from that of Marx), it was largely the moral ideal of equality that drove them on, and led to the economic and social structures that they put in place. Agriculture in Israel had hitherto depended on the employment of cheap Arab labour. Within the Kibbutz movement the extremely hard labour of claiming the inhospitable land for cultivation was the joint responsibility of those men and women who had voluntarily undertaken 'to make the desert flower'. The duties

---

[1] For a detailed and fascinating account of one such community, in rural Oregon, see chapter 4 of Frances FitzGerald, *Cities on a Hill* (Simon & Schuster, London and New York 1986). She notes that many of those who joined were not teenagers, but had been affluent professionals, who gave up their possessions in exchange for manual labour in the commune.

of domestic work, including the care and education of the children of the Kibbutz were also shared. The Hebrew terms for 'husband' and 'wife' were not used of couples, on the grounds that the word for 'wife' carried an unacceptable connotation of being among the possessions of her husband, as, in the Ten Commandments, she is so included, along with the ox and the ass and 'any thing that is his'. The children of these couples lived together in a 'children's house', a kind of year-through boarding school, though there was contact with their parents for part of each day. Their education was carried out by members of the community, and they were not encouraged to go outside, even for higher education. However, after the Second World War it became increasingly common for the State of Israel, which now subsidised the Kibbutzim, to pay the university fees of those members who wished to apply. For by now the Kibbutzim had long ceased to be entirely agricultural, and had branched out into industry, including pharmaceuticals and the manufacture of armaments.

There are still more than two hundred Kibbutzim in Israel, mostly clustered round the Sea of Galilee where the movement started. But their position has become increasingly ambiguous. For, though receiving commissions and subsidies from the state, they are in theory still jointly owned by those who are born, live and work there. As they become more 'normal', and more money flows in and out, so the allocation of jobs within each community becomes more professional, with qualified engineers, trained teachers and trained chefs taking their appropriate responsibilities, women more often taking on domestic and 'caring' jobs. More external workers are employed, who are paid varying wages according to the nature of their jobs, and who are not members of the Kibbutz. And so the Kibbutzim have been fairly thoroughly commercialised, some even running as hotels. It follows that there is growing dissatisfaction over the question of ownership. Many kibbutzniks, as they grow up, qualify for the professions, such as medicine and the law, and wish to buy themselves out, to pursue careers where the best opportunities are open to them. But what do they now own? And is it not still their responsibility to continue to work within what was originally their own tightly-knit community? Once a first-generation community has produced a second and further generations, it seems to me that such questions are bound to arise, and to produce increasing conflict and litigation. The original community agreed to hold everything in common for the good of the whole, and for the sake of the life they had chosen to live. But could such an agreement be binding on their children and grandchildren? The problems raised are akin to those raised about political sovereignty, for those philosophers who relied on the original contract as the source of legitimate government. To what extent could such a contract be held to be binding on future people? As we have seen, Hume for one held that, even if such a contract had originally been made, it could have no force to bind people in perpetuity.

It seems to me inevitable that, if the Kibbutz movement survives, it can do so only in an attenuated form, and will become no more than an example of the last kind of common ownership that I shall consider, namely employee ownership. I shall examine this kind of collective ownership in some detail, because it brings out what is a crucial part of the concept of ownership itself, indeed perhaps its defining core, namely the idea of responsibility for what is owned, along with a genuine desire that it should flourish, and be something we are proud of. This is what we feel when we own a horse, a house or, as we have seen, a garden. It is the existential nature of ownership.

In 2011, the UK government, in the person of the deputy prime minister, commissioned a review of employee ownership which was carried out by Graeme Nuttall, and published the following year.[2] Nuttall found conclusive evidence that employee ownership, when it constituted a substantial part of the ownership of a company (anything above 25 per cent) and when it was combined with full knowledge of and participation in the management of the company, increased productivity, made for greater resilience in hard times, increased the wellbeing of the workforce and decreased the turnover of staff. These successes were especially marked in small companies, employing 75 members of staff or fewer, but could also be seen in much larger organisations. The obstacles standing in the way of more employee ownership were largely a matter of ignorance. Government departments were therefore encouraged to raise the general awareness of the possibilities; for example, when a founder/owner of a company was contemplating retirement, advice

---

[2] *Sharing Success: The Nuttall Review of Employee Ownership* (Crown Copyright, London 2012).

should be readily available, not only from the Employee Ownership Association, but from independent accountants and tax advisers as well. The Review helpfully sets out the steps needed to achieve employee ownership in such a case. Nuttall was a great enthusiast, as was Nick Clegg, the deputy prime minister, who commissioned the review.

Perhaps in consequence of the publication of the Nuttall Report, the year 2013 brought some notoriety to employee ownership, on account of an ill-conceived attempt by the Coalition government, encouraged by the Treasury, to give help to start-up companies by enabling them to offer shares to their employees, in exchange for which those employees would sacrifice some of their benefits, including entitlement to paid maternity leave, and the right to further training at the expense of the company. This scheme was outlined by the Chancellor of the Exchequer, George Osborne, at the party conference in 2012, and incorporated in a Bill entitled the Enterprise and Regulatory Reform Bill, which was subjected to severe criticism in the House of Lords in April 2013. When the proposal had first been announced, it had been referred to by the government as 'Employee Ownership'. However it was widely, and in my view rightly, criticised as constituting a thoroughly bad deal for employees, who were being asked to forgo hard-won rights in exchange for a highly risky stake in the company in the form of shares for which they themselves had to pay, and which would very probably lead to loss rather than profit. Moreover, the Association of Employee Ownership, a network of more than a hundred companies, objected to their name being associated in any way with the scheme, since their member companies aim to offer joint ownership to all their employees with no loss of rights. The scheme, it was pointed out, would be highly divisive, when some employees enjoyed rights that were denied to others, who would in effect be paying for the benefits of their fellow workers. In any case, any employee who accepted such a deal would be an insane risk-taker. Government spokesmen floundered in their defence of the plan, adding a clause to the effect that employees who were minded to take up the offer of shares should not proceed without impartial financial advice. But who was to pay for such advice? That was never made clear.

In their defence, it could be said that, in putting forward their proposals, the government probably had in mind some small high-tech companies, increasingly being started up in industrial parks outside university towns such as Cambridge and Bath, where finances are precarious, and where the rights of employees, secured by their unions, might be unduly burdensome. However, in such companies the distinction between employees and owners is already blurred; those who work in them are highly skilled colleagues, the companies being more collegiate than commercial. Such companies are often not completely unionised, and probably have fairly informal arrangements about holidays and other perks. So they hardly need the new scheme; when they start to make profit, if they ever do, they are usually sold or otherwise absorbed into bigger firms, and the joint owners are free to start again, or to work for larger organisations if they so wish.

However this may be, the government refused to withdraw the provision, claiming to expect hundreds if not thousands of applications from companies to join the scheme before the summer was over. Fortunately the term 'employee ownership' was quietly dropped. By July 2013 four companies had expressed possible interest in the scheme, and two had followed up with requests for information. The press unanimously declared it a flop, though the Act remains on the Statute Book.

As to real employee ownership, that is, ownership of a stake in a company without consequential loss of employment rights, the largest and probably the best-known example of this in the UK is the John Lewis Partnership, the enormously flourishing outcome of the vision of its founder, John Spedan Lewis. He set up the partnership after the death of his father in 1928. His father, John Lewis, had bought several shops in London, including the draper's shop which bore his name in Oxford Street, and which became a very successful department store, through his importing cloth from the Far East, especially from India. But John Lewis's two sons disapproved of the way the business was run, and of the miserable conditions, low wages and lack of security suffered by the employees. Spedan Lewis, having left public school, started to work for his father when he was nineteen, and on his twenty-first birthday was given another of his father's shops, Peter Jones in Sloane Square. Here, though not for a time making much profit, he started to put into effect some of the ideas which later informed the partnership. He started an employees' committee where their voices could be heard; and in general he began to improve their working conditions. When his father died (having accumulated enormous wealth, but spent almost none of it) the two shops were joined in one partnership, with John Spedan as its chairman, a post he occupied until 1963 when he was succeeded by his nephew, Peter Lewis. The principles on which the partnership was founded have changed extraordinarily little up to the present day. The chairman is now a former professional soldier, an officer in the Brigade of Guards, and later a businessman with connections in the Far East, Sir Charles Mayfield, who is the first non-member of the family to lead it.

In his autobiography (privately printed in 1952), Spedan Lewis set out his firm belief that it was possible to have as one's first consideration the wellbeing and happiness of one's staff, and yet make a business profitable. Indeed, the two kinds of success stood or failed together. He quoted many partners who, on being called up and obliged to leave the partnership in the Second World War, expressed their sadness at doing so, their enjoyment of the atmosphere of their place of work, and their feeling that not only did the company belong to them, but they to the company, in the sense in which one may belong to one's college, or one's regiment.

The Founder, as he was known, was insistent on genuine partnership, and that meant genuine participation in the decision making of the company. Communication between workers at all levels was therefore of the highest importance. Even while he was still at Peter Jones, Lewis started the *Gazette*, an in-house periodical which is still published, and to which all partners in all of the stores can contribute articles and opinions. The present chairman is equally insistent that mere ownership of shares in a company will bring no improvements if partners are not kept fully informed both about how the company is performing and about what future plans are being considered, to which plans they may contribute their input, since each store elects a representative on the Council, which in turn is represented on the board. The Council has some real powers, notably the power to dismiss the chairman of the board. But it has powers also to decide what charities the partnership will support, and to what extent. There is no chief executive officer; the chairman of the board fulfils that function. There is no pretence that all partners are equal: their salaries are differentiated according to the nature of their work (and they still need their trades unions, to support them in cases of alleged unfair dismissal, and other such matters).

According to Sir Charles Mayfield, who has been most generous of his time in discussing and explaining the partnership, what makes it work so well is that all the partnership shares are held in trust for the partners. The trustees are a small body, not more than three or four including the chairman. It is their responsibility to distribute any bonuses to the partners each year; and since the trust is for the benefit of the partnership, it cannot use money for any other purpose, nor can the board take a sudden decision to sell the company. This contributes, according to Sir Charles, both to the continuity of the partnership, and to the possibility of riding commercial and economic storms, as well as to the sense of security of the individual workers. (Such an arrangement, of shares held in trust, was that most favoured by the Nuttall Review.)

John Spedan Lewis, in a broadcast talk delivered in 1957, expressed the view that the pattern of partnership, or worker ownership (he rejected the concept of 'employee' in this context) was perhaps the only alternative to communism in the world of post-war Britain. Sir Charles Mayfield, however, does not regard it as a panacea, and concedes that it might not suit all kinds of commerce or industry. But he values it very highly, and thoroughly believes in the increased sense of responsibility for the success of the company that partnership brings. I witnessed this myself in a small way when in 1990 I was asked by Peter Lewis, then chairman of the partnership, to speak at the AGM and dinner, held in the restaurant at the top of Peter Jones (the invitation was a quid pro quo. I had sought financial help for Girton College, of which I was then Mistress, relying on the fact that the Founder and his wife had been generous to the college in the past. Instead of money, Peter Lewis had sent his expert in apples from the Waitrose orchards in Kent to help the college restock its orchard of old and rare apple trees). I was able in my speech to expand, sincerely, on the glories of the Waitrose in Marlborough, then my local town, which had converted even my husband to shopping, something he had refused to do before. But I had already heard Peter Lewis explain that this had been a bad year, and that there would be no bonuses. I was astonished to hear the response of those present: 'Well! We'll just have to do better next year'. I had not realised until then how seriously the partners took their ownership of the firm.

My friend, the surviving member of the British Communist Party, was scornful when I told him this story: 'None of the cleaners is a partner' was his response. And that is true. The partners are selected to work in the shops and connected aspects of the business as people likely to be willing to undergo training, and to commit themselves to the success of the enterprise. Their selection and training is careful and expensive. They are by no means casual workers. But I have no doubt that a cleaner who aspired to become a partner could apply to do so, and would be accepted provided he showed commitment. And it is remarkable how many casual Saturday workers, students from sixth forms and university, do indeed go on to seek full-time employment and partnership later on.

So I believe that the John Lewis Partnership, and other similar companies such as the engineering and construction firm Arup, and the large and extraordinarily competent removal firm, G.B. Liners, on the whole succeed in doing what John Spedan Lewis proposed, that is improve the life of those who work in them and make the companies profitable through fostering a sense of ownership in each individual.

But it must be conceded that it is the sense of ownership, rather than ownership itself that makes the difference, at least among those working for the John Lewis Partnership. They are called partners, and they feel that the company is theirs; but critics point out that they have no proprietary ownership of their shares and they cannot buy or sell them at will. Nor can they decide to dissolve or sell the company. To sceptics it may appear to be a success story built on an illusion. Mayfield of course concedes that partners have no right to sell their shares (or the company itself); and that the right to dispose of a thing is normally entailed by owning it. But in the case where the shares that are owned are held in trust, the absence of a right to sell does not make the common ownership unreal. When I asked Sir Charles about this apparent deficiency in the normal rights of ownership, he said that the responsibility of ownership was the more genuine because the shares were held in trust for the benefit of the partners. The absence of the right to sell actually contributed to that responsibility, and thus, of course, to the stability of the partnership. He incidentally pointed out that Germany has many times more such employee-owned companies than the UK, and that this may be thought to have contributed to the stability of the German economy as a whole, even through the tremors shaking the rest of the eurozone.

Even if the John Lewis Partnership now numbers over 70,000 workers who are largely content with their lot and take pride in their work, this is of course an extremely modest achievement compared with what communism aimed for. But its very modesty is what makes it relevant to the examination of ownership. If it is the sense of ownership that generates a sense of responsibility for the flourishing of an enterprise, we are forced to ask how widely this sense of ownership can, realistically, be extended. Environmentalists and Green parties want us to take responsibility for the whole planet. Since we cannot even pretend to own it all (this would truly be, as they say, 'Playing God'), in the next chapters we shall consider some of the ways that have been proposed to make us take on such global responsibility, without which, it is argued, the earth will become uninhabitable and life will disappear. However, before pursuing this line of enquiry, it is necessary to return, as I promised, to the aesthetic and emotional matters with which we ended chapter 3. For whether or not we can embrace within our sense of responsibility the planet as a whole depends in large part on our emotional attitude towards the natural world, and this we must explore further, and beyond the confines of the garden.

6. The unowned: the romantic idea of wilderness

Let us turn back now, as I promised, to chapter 3. There I considered some aspects of gardening, and I hope to have shown that the essence of gardening is to claim, or reclaim, a plot of land, to attach it to oneself and make it serve some human purpose, whether utilitarian or aesthetic. It is thus ownership in action; and this is as true of the small plot belonging to a cottage as it is of the rolling parklands that surround a mansion. But alongside the desire to tame and improve nature, and more or less contemporary with that particularly painterly approach to the improvement of property which saw it primarily as something to be looked at, as picturesque, there was a growing and near-contradictory sense that nature is almost sacred, and should as far as possible be left alone. There was a growing belief that the intervention of man to improve nature in fact inevitably despoils it. Jean-Jacques Rousseau, that alleged progenitor of the French Revolution, became notorious also for the first expression of such ideas. His first publication of them was in his entry for a prize essay competition, in 1754, entitled *The Discourse of the Origin of Inequality among Men*, in which he attempted to look back to a time when men lived in a state of nature; but he elaborated them far more influentially in his two novels, which achieved huge popularity in pre-revolutionary Paris. The first of these novels, *La Nouvelle Héloise*, was about a girl whose story is played out through her emotions and her sensibilities, rather than her reason. She is a kind of prototype of Jane Austen's Marianne. The second, *Émile*, is a detailed prescription for the education of young children, through the story of a boy educated within his family, and allowed the freedom to develop his sense of the world through constant contact with nature. The only book Émile was allowed to read until he was twelve years old was Daniel Defoe's *Robinson Crusoe* (presumably someone at some stage taught him to read, for he can hardly have picked up the skill from the trees and flowers and animals among which he spent his life).

Robinson Crusoe (published in 1719) could be read as a moral tale of a human being's direct immersion in untamed nature, with no intermediary buying and selling, no guidance but human need, and all the lessons about how to live coming from nature itself. And this was to be the essence of Émile's education.

It is astonishing to reflect how strong and lasting an influence this book, a thoroughly philosophical novel, has had on educational theory since it was first published in 1762 (in which year it was also publicly burned in Switzerland, because it was hostile to institutional religion; its being banned doubtless adding to its fame). Johann Heinrich Pestalozzi took over many of Rousseau's ideas and worked out his educational theories in numerous institutions for the education of the poor. He held that the powers of attention, observation and memory must be developed before those of judgement, and that education must be of the 'eye, hand and heart'. Then Friedrich Wilhelm Froebel came, as a tutor to two young German aristocrats, to stay for two years in one of these Pestalozzi institutions, and was to take over his theories of free, outdoor, activity-based education for young children. He established many schools of his own, and Froebel training and Froebel schools flourished all over Europe, with their own training colleges, well into the twentieth century. The last of these colleges now forms the Education Department of the University of Roehampton in London. Later still, Maria Montessori developed the Montessori Method of teaching young children, concentrating on giving them the maximum sensory experience, including the development of the sense of touch, and Montessori schools flourished in the USA and UK. The method is still influential, especially in the education of children with dyslexia. Maria Montessori acknowledged her immense debt to Rousseau.

In the UK the controversial Plowden Report on primary education in the UK was published in 1967, the work of a committee chaired by Bridget Plowden, herself a school rebel, and a great lover of Rousseauesque ideas of free outdoor education, and as little time as possible sitting at desks within the restrictions of the classroom. This report has often been blamed for the destruction of primary school standards, and of the discipline of the 'three Rs', putting in its place child-centred, 'discovery' methods which abandoned such tools as the multiplication tables to be learned by rote and rhythm. This is doubtless an exaggeration; but the ideas of the teacher as 'facilitator', a neutral 'enabler', like Émile's tutor, was undoubtedly fashionable in teacher-training colleges in the 1960s and 1970s; and so the ideas trickled down for many years into a number of primary schools. At the same time there grew up a whole vocabulary of horticultural metaphors in the discussion of the education of young children, who must have space to grow and spread in order to blossom, who must not have their natural growth stunted by too ruthless pruning and training, who flower only in an environment suited to their needs. All this, sometimes for good, often for ill, we owe to Rousseau.

And, of course, to romanticism; for such language is the child of the romantic movement, and Rousseau was in some sense the founding father of that movement, which introduced an entirely new attitude to man's relation with nature, and especially with what we think of as 'the country'. For the first time, uncultivated nature began to be thought of as something good and valuable in itself. In his *Journey to the Western Islands of Scotland*, published in 1773, Samuel Johnson described a horrendous journey through the Isle of Mull, in which, not really knowing how large the unmapped island was, he, with the ever-optimistic James Boswell, proposed to travel from Tobermory to Iona on horseback in about eight hours (it takes a good three hours by bus today, on excellent roads). He was appalled by what he saw:

> We travelled many hours through a tract, black and barren, in which, however, there were the reliques of humanity; for we found a ruined chapel in our way. It is natural, in travelling this gloom of desolation, to inquire whether something may not be done to give nature a more cheerful face, and whether those hills and moors that afford heath cannot with a little care and labour bear something better?

His first thought was that someone should plant trees. The misery of their journey 'was not balanced by any gratification of the eye or mind. We were now long enough acquainted with hills and heath to have lost the emotions, whether pleasant or painful, that they once raised'. So much for the glories of the mountains and wildlife of Mull. Three years later, writing of what it is that constitutes a picturesque landscape, William Gilpin wrote:

> The generality of people find . . . wild country in its natural state totally unpleasing. There are few who do not prefer the busy scenes of

> cultivation to the greatest of Nature's rough productions. In general, indeed, when we meet with a description of a pleasing country, we hear of haycocks or waving cornfields or labourers at their plough.[1]

Of course the rugged mountainsides had their charms, but, as we have seen, strictly as a backdrop to the figures at the front of the scene.

Is it, then, that, in aesthetic theory, romanticism brought the sublime into fashion at the expense of the beautiful, the tamed giving place to the wild? This would be to oversimplify a bit. The words 'beautiful' 'picturesque' and 'sublime' are all of them items in the vocabulary of taste, or the language of criticism. The romantic concept of nature as an intrinsic good is not really part of this discourse, though closely connected with it. To understand this we must go back to the original distinction between the beautiful and the sublime.

The concept of the sublime comes from a Greek treatise of doubtful date and authorship, ascribed to Longinus, though whether a Longinus known to have been an historian living in the third century or an otherwise unknown writer living a century or so earlier is not entirely clear (given the authors he quotes, and does not quote, the earlier date is more probable). The ascription may simply have been the result of a clerical error. The treatise is entitled *peri Hypsou*, (About the High), and when it was translated into Latin 'the High' became '*sublimus*', the sublime. This was a word that had been used in the Augustan period by Horace in his literary criticism, not only of style but of some aspects of nature, deemed by him fit to be written about in such a style. Etymologists think that the word derives from the words 'sub' and 'limen'. The limen is literally the top beam of a door, but the word is used metaphorically for an entry or threshold to something out of reach. At any rate the treatise, of which parts are missing, is concerned with rhetorical style, and is full of examples from both orators, such as Demosthenes and Cicero, and poets, such as Homer and Sappho. It has many examples, too, of failed attempts at sublimity of style, which are pompous, tedious, ridiculous or over the top. However, true sublimity, so the argument

---

[1] W. Gilpin (1779), Observations, Relative Chiefly to Picturesque Beauty, Made in the Year 1776, On Several Parts of Great Britain; Particularly the High-Lands of Scotland, Volume II, Section XXI, p. 111.

goes, arises from the elevation and moral loftiness of the thought that lies behind it, and this nobility of ideas spills out into the words. A sublime style thus comes from a noble character, and is not something that can easily be taught. But it is instantly recognisable, by the effect it has on the hearer or reader. Two passages are worth quoting: 'It is natural in us to feel our souls lifted up by the true sublime . . . to be filled with joy and pride, as though we ourselves had originated the ideas we read', and 'When a passage is pregnant with suggestion; when it is hard, nay impossible, to distract the attention from it; and when it takes a strong and lasting hold on the memory, then we may be sure that we have lighted on the true sublime'. We recognise the sublime, in short, by inner feeling; yet we are prepared to identify it as something outside ourselves, objectively present in the passage we are reading, which is the cause of that feeling.

We may perhaps compare this way of identifying the 'true sublime' with A.E. Housman's criterion for judging whether something is 'pure' poetry. In the Leslie Stephen Lecture for 1933, Housman took as his subject 'The Name and Nature of Poetry'. True poetry, he argues, can be recognised, but not defined. And it is recognised, in his case, by the physiological effects that it has upon him, the shiver down his spine and the tears in his eyes. These symptoms are sometimes, but not, he holds, always, accompanied by a recognition of the truth or profundity of the thought expressed. He quotes as example 'six simple words of Milton, "Nymphs and Shepherds, dance no more"', and asks:

> What is it that can draw tears, as I know it can, to the eyes of more readers than one? What in the world is there to cry about? Why have the mere words the physical effects of pathos, when the sense of the passage is blithe and gay? I can only say, because they are poetry, and find their way to something in man that is obscure and latent, something older than the present organisation of his nature, like the patches of fen which still linger here and there in the drained lands of Cambridgeshire.

And later he says: 'Experience has taught me, when I am shaving in the morning, to keep watch over my thoughts, because if a line of poetry strays into my mind my skin bristles so that the razor will not act'. His next example is perhaps even closer to Longinus's concept of the sublime. He quotes from William Blake: 'Tho' thou art Worship'd by the Names Divine. / Of Jesus & Jehovah, thou art still / The Son of Morn in weary Night's decline, / The lost Traveller's

Dream under the Hill'. And he says 'It purports to be theology; what theological sense it may have, if any, I cannot imagine and have no wish to learn; it is pure and self-existent poetry, which leaves no room in me for anything else besides'. I agree with Housman. There are passages that I cannot read or hear without shivers in my legs and tears in my eyes. Even copying out those lines of Blake produced the physical effect. It is because the passage is, in Longinus's words, 'pregnant with suggestion' that we are thus moved. For the words are not mere sounds, though they are sounds as well. They are not nonsense, like the Jabberwock. They have their own connotations, and these resonate for us in the sounds.

Housman, like Longinus, was concerned with art, the art of the written or spoken word. It was perhaps David Hartley who first examined the notion of sublimity in the context not of art but of nature itself. He was a practising physician, and in 1749 published an ambitious work entitled *Observations on Man, his Frame, his Duty and his Expectations*. In it he combined a psychological theory of the association of ideas with an attempt at a physiological account of the brain. In proposition xciv of the *Observations*, he wrote:

> [T]here being a precipice, a cataract, a mountain of snow etc. in one part of the scene, the nascent ideas of fear and horror magnify and enliven all the other ideas and by degrees pass into pleasures suggesting the security from pain. In like manner, the grandeur of some scenes, and the novelty of others, by exciting surprise and wonder i.e. by making a great difference in the preceding and subsequent states of mind so as to border upon or even enter the limits of pain, may greatly enhance the pleasure.

Hartley was an influential writer (Samuel Taylor Coleridge at one time professed himself a follower, and named his eldest son after him); and 'the association of ideas' became part of the vocabulary of psychology. What is relevant to our investigation is the transition, in the debate about the sublime, from the sphere of style to that of the reaction to nature itself.

Edmund Burke in 1757 published his contribution to the ongoing debate in his *Philosophical Enquiry into the Sublime and the Beautiful*, and he followed Hartley in identifying fear as the prime constituent of the recognition of the sublime: 'The passion caused by the great and the sublime in Nature is astonishment . . . and astonishment is that state of the soul in which all its motions are suspended with some degree of horror' and 'In this case the mind is so entirely filled with its object that it cannot entertain any other'.[2] Thus the sublime is entirely different from the beautiful, because its physiological causes are opposite. The sense of the sublime arises from pain, the appreciation of beauty from pleasure.

In 1764 Immanuel Kant published an examination of Burke's theory in his *Observations as to the Feelings of the Beautiful and the Sublime*; but his full examination of the distinction came in the *Critique of Judgment*. In this, the last of his three critiques, he brought man's relationship with nature into the great epistemological framework which he had sought to establish in the first two critiques, the *Critique of Pure Reason*, concerned with knowledge, and the *Critique of Practical Reason*, concerned with action and morality. The *Critique of Judgement* deals with two facets of man and nature, that of nature study, or the biological sciences, and that of aesthetics.

In the first critique, the *Critique of Pure Reason*, Kant had undertaken to prove that the knowledge we have of the world can come to us only through the senses, through which we become acquainted with the appearances of things, their visual, auditory and tactual aspects. So far he was in agreement with both Locke and Hume. However, he held that these appearances are necessarily ordered and rendered intelligible, predictable and capable of generalisation by certain fixed and necessary concepts of the imagination and understanding, concepts employed by each individual 'I' or 'self', which is the 'vehicle of all concepts'. Yet they are shared by all, according to rules of logic, which are themselves unchangeable and cannot be otherwise. These concepts are known as the 'Categories of the Understanding'. If there were no such contribution from the perceiving mind, experience would be nothing but an incoherent, constantly changing chaos of fluctuating impressions. But we know that it is not so. We in fact confidently apply such concepts or categories as that of cause or continuing, separate substantial existence to the things that we perceive, and this is how we understand them. Fortunately I need not go into the question whether this framework, which, Kant argued, the mind imposes on the world of experience, is the only possible framework, as he claims to prove. The relevance

[2] Edmund Burke, *Philosophical Enquiry into the Sublime and the Beautiful* (1757), p. 58.

for my purpose is to emphasise that Kant was concerned with how we order the appearances of things, not things themselves. Yet such things (things-in-themselves) must exist, independently of our minds. For he argues that to speak of appearances without supposing anything of which they are appearances would be nonsensical.[3] Of these things-in-themselves, however, which lie behind our experience, we can have no concept, and therefore no understanding or scientific knowledge whatever. Yet despite this, he says, we can think them; they are 'noumena'. Indeed we can think whatever we choose, as long as we avoid contradictory thoughts (for our minds are determined by logic). These indefinite thoughts that we have are called the 'Ideas of Reason', quite different from the Concepts of the Understanding, yet exerting an influence on our behaviour, our character and our whole life.

Kant's great conceptual framework of the critiques was conceived partly in order to allay the fears aroused by his predecessor David Hume, that one must be completely sceptical as to the veracity of sense experience. Like Descartes, though by a different route, Hume held that it is impossible ever to prove that things in the world have any independent existence at all, since all that we have is an endlessly changing series of sense-impressions and ideas in our minds, between which there are no real connections, but only those that we habitually imagine. We cannot get behind them to the world beyond them. When afflicted by such radical scepticism, Hume had simply to stop thinking about it, and join friends in a game of backgammon. Kant's great reassurance was built on his supposition that we can know truths about what we perceive because we partly construct these things ourselves. He argues that our minds do not merely receive impressions passively, but rather they actively contribute to the ordering and predictability of these Impressions, according to necessary laws of logic. And since the mind of every rational creature is determined by the same logic, we can be certain that we share our world with other rational beings, and need not fall into the solipsism or scepticism to which Hume was prey.

And there was another great fear that Kant sought to lay to rest, which had been aroused this time by Isaac Newton, namely that the

---

[3] Immanuel Kant, *Critique of Pure Reason*, Preface to 2nd edn (1787) Bxxvii and footnote.

world, including the world of human behaviour, might be totally explicable in terms of physical laws of nature. Such materialism would leave no room for human autonomy, and thus no room for morality. Yet, Kant argued, we are all conscious that there is a difference between doing what is right, fulfilling a duty, and neglecting to do so. We are thus aware of our own freedom to choose between them, and we know that that freedom entails that we may choose to obey a moral imperative, or to disregard it in favour of our own desires and interests. This consciousness of freedom is called an 'Idea of Reason'; it is something by which we live, which dictates our choices and aspirations, but of which the scientific understanding can give us no exact knowledge. Freedom is exercised by us in making for ourselves a moral law that will govern right conduct for everyone who is capable of exercising reason. It is, for each person, his own moral law which is yet binding, like the laws of logic, on all rational beings. And each rational being knows this freedom from within.

The American psychologist and philosopher, William James, who did not hold Kant in very high esteem, explains it thus:

> . . . Kant held a curious doctrine about such objects of belief as God, the design of creation, the soul, its freedom and the life hereafter [all of them Ideas of Reason]. These things, he said, were properly not objects of knowledge at all. Our conceptions always require a sense-content to work with, and as the words 'soul', 'God', 'immortality' cover no distinctive sense-content whatever, it follows that theoretically speaking they are words devoid of any significance. Yet strangely enough they have a definite meaning for our practice. We can act as if there were a God . . . consider Nature as if she were full of special designs; lay plans as if we were to be immortal; and we find then that these words make a definite difference in our moral lives . . . So we have the strange phenomenon, as Kant assures us, of the mind believing with all its strength in the real presence of a set of things of no one of which it can form any notion whatever.

And he goes on:

> My object in recalling Kant's doctrine to your mind is not to express any opinion of the accuracy of this particularly uncouth part of his philosophy, but only to illustrate the characteristic of human nature we are considering [that is, the propensity to religious experiences] by an example so classical in its exaggeration. The sentiment of reality can indeed attach itself so strongly to our object of belief that our life is polarised through

> and through, so to speak, by its sense of the reality of the thing believed in, and yet that thing, for purposes of definite description, can hardly be said to be present to our mind at all. It is as if a bar of iron, without touch or sight, with no representative faculty whatever, might nevertheless be strongly endowed with an inner capacity for magnetic feeling; and as if, through the various arousals of its magnetism by magnets coming and going in its neighbourhood, it might be consciously determined to different attitudes and tendencies. Such a bar of iron could never give you an outward description of the agencies that had the power of stirring it so strongly; yet of their presence, and their significance for its life, it would be intensely aware, through every fibre of its being.[4]

Kant concludes the second critique, the *Critique of Practical Reason*, with these words: 'Two things fill the mind with ever-increasing wonder and awe, the more often and the more intensely the mind of thought is drawn to them: the starry heavens above and the moral law within me'. 'The moral law within me' had been the subject matter of the second critique and stands for the idea of freedom. 'The starry heavens above' stand for that aspect of the sublime, already familiar in the contemporary critical literature, characterised as 'the vast' in nature. This is where Kant prepares for his third critique, where he considers the human engagement with nature itself. He starts with the idea that in studying nature, investigators treat the notion of purpose as a kind of methodological device. He has already, in the first critique, dismissed the notion that we can have actual knowledge of God, or of any purpose he had in creating the universe and its contents. Yet scientists of nature nevertheless tend to ask of, for example, a part of a bird's wing, what is it for? What function does it have in flight? They conduct their enquiries, that is, as if there were a purpose in all natural objects. This device is especially useful in the biological, as opposed to the physical or chemical sciences.

The second part of the critique is devoted to the other aspect of our connection with nature, the aesthetic. Here the idea of purpose is invoked again in the analysis of what it is for a natural object, or indeed any other object or artefact, to be judged beautiful. Kant accepts the common view, expounded by Burke among others, that the beautiful is pleasurable. We receive the particular kind of

[4] William James, *The Varieties of Religious Experience* (Penguin Classics, New York 1985) pp. 54–6.

pleasure that is the recognition of beauty from any object which in a different way seems to be purposive, this time to be moving towards some preordained end which we can imaginatively comprehend, although in fact the thing in question has no purpose. We comprehend in our imagination the direction, the shape, form or pattern that the object has, whether it is a natural or an artificial object. A melody for instance, whether composed by a human being or spontaneously uttered by a blackbird, may have a cadence that we can foresee (though blackbirds often let us down by failing to get it 'right' at the end. And in any case part of the pleasure in birdsong, especially that of thrushes and nightingales, is the purely sensory softness and clearness of the sound whether there is pattern to be found in it or not. This has always been part of the observation of those philosophers, including Kant himself, who have sought to define the beautiful).

Kant agrees with his predecessors and contemporaries in distinguishing absolutely our experience of formal beauty from that of the sublime. But, characteristically, he draws the distinction more systematically, to fit in with the architecture of the other critiques. In the first place, while starting, like Burke, from the effects on us of nature rather than of art, he links the two aspects of the discussion together through the concept of genius. The nature of genius had been as much discussed by critics before Kant, as had that of taste. Hume, for example, had identified a man of genius as one who more than most men 'allows his imagination to run from one end of the universe to the other in collecting those ideas that belong to any subject'; and he described this ability to collect together relevant and illuminating ideas, which ordinary people would not have thought of, as 'a kind of magic faculty of the soul, inexplicable by the utmost efforts of the human understanding'.[5] Kant joined the concept of genius with his ideas of reason, and both with the sublime. A man of genius, though even he cannot by the utmost stretch of the imagination conjure up images of the ideas of reason, as we can conjure up images of appearances in the world as organised by the understanding, yet, recognising that whatever is sublime in nature suggests or reminds us of ideas of reason, this man of genius will attempt to express them directly. What the artist does is 'to create a second

[5] David Hume, *Treatise* Bk 1 part 1 section vii.

Nature' which may give rise to the sense of sublimity, just as nature itself may give rise to such a sense. Kant defines genius as 'the faculty of presenting Aesthetic Ideas'.[6] And in the same paragraph an aesthetic idea is defined as 'a representation of the imagination which induces much thought; yet without the possibility of any definite thought, that is concept, being adequate to it'. The aesthetic ideas with which great art confronts us are 'representations which strain after something lying beyond experience'.[7]

Kant's account of the role of artistic genius, then, as it were, tidies up the long tradition starting with Longinus of hovering between nature and representations of nature, as instancing the sublime. A writer, composer or artist of genius can produce work which, like nature itself, can give us ideas that are 'pregnant with suggestion'. For aesthetic ideas like ideas of reason can never be wholly explicit, nor wholly adequate. The imagination is left feeling there is something beyond it which it cannot reach.

Kant held that it is nature itself that brings us closest to the realisation of man's loftiest faculty, reason, that which sets him above all the rest of nature. Here is how he puts it:

> Bold, overhanging and threatening rocks, thunder-clouds piled up the vault of heaven, borne along with flashes and peals, volcanos in all their violence of destruction, hurricanes leaving desolation in their track, the boundless ocean rising in rebellious force, the high waterfall of some mighty river make our power of resistance of small moment in comparison to their might. But, provided our position is secure, their aspect is all the more attractive for their fearfulness; and we readily call these objects sublime because they raise the forces of the soul above the vulgar commonplace, and discover within us a power of quite another kind, which gives us courage to be able to measure ourselves against the seeming omnipotence of Nature. In the immeasurableness of Nature, and the incompetence of our faculty for adopting a standard proportionate to the aesthetic estimation of the magnitude of its realm we find our own limitation. But, with this, we also find in our rational faculty another, non-sensuous standard, one which has that infinity itself under it, and in comparison with which everything in nature is small: and so we find in our minds a pre-eminence over nature, in its immeasurability. Now in just the same way the irresistibility of nature forces upon us the recognition of our physical helplessness as beings of nature, but at the same time reveals a faculty of estimating ourselves as independent of nature

[6] *Critique of Judgment* 314.
[7] Ibid.

> and discovers a pre-eminence over nature that is the foundation of self-preservation of quite another kind from that which may be assailed and brought into danger by external nature. This saves humanity in our own person from humiliation, even though as mortal men we may have to submit to violence.[8]

The recognition of the sublime in nature lies in its reminder of the moral law within. Nature itself is interpreted as revealing, or partly revealing, the supreme truth about humanity: that human beings, and they alone, are capable of moral autonomy.

This thought, 'uncouth', perhaps, and certainly convoluted, filters down to become part of what we may think of as the central romantic view of nature. We see this most clearly in the work of that great romantic, Samuel Taylor Coleridge. Of Coleridge's theory of imagination, John Stuart Mill wrote: 'He was anticipated in all his doctrines by the great Germans of the latter half of the last century . . . He was the creator rather of the shape in which it has appeared among us than of the doctrine itself'.[9] There seems no reason to disagree. We know that Coleridge was a voracious reader, and of a magpie disposition, picking up and appropriating anything that he found to confirm or deepen his own often 'half-formed' thoughts. We know too that he was not careful about attributing his ideas to their sources, often copying into his notebooks long passages from German philosophers, and later using them as his own. His *Biographia Literaria* of 1817 contains long passages from the philosopher and critic, Friedrich Schelling, unascribed. However, it is not with allegations of plagiarism that I am here concerned, but with the way in which, whatever its origins, the view of nature, wild unimproved nature, as intrinsically one of the greatest goods for mankind gradually spread, and became what I suspect is an immovable undercurrent in the thought of the Western world.

Coleridge started to read the German philosophers in 1801 when he was confined to his room, suffering the acute effects of opium addiction. When he recovered from his illness, he went for a long solitary walk, climbing Scafell Pike, the highest peak in the Lake District. In his descent, he found himself on a ledge of rock from which he could for some time find no way down. Later, having

---

8 Ibid., p. 450.

9 J.S. Mill, *Dissertations and Discussions* reprinted by Chatto & Windus as *Mill on Bentham and Coleridge* ed. F.R. Leavis 1950.

somehow rescued himself, he described what happened in a letter to his beloved 'Asra' (Sara Hutchinson) in terms that are purely (even absurdly) Kantian:

> My Limbs were all a-tremble. I lay on my Back to rest myself, and began according to my custom to laugh at myself for a Madman, when the sight of the Crags above me on each side, and the impetuous Clouds just over them, posting themselves so luridly and so rapidly northward, overawed me. I lay in a state of almost prophetic Trance and Delight – and blessed God aloud for the powers of Reason and the Will, which remaining, no danger can overpower us! O God, I exclaimed aloud, how calm, how blessed am I now: I know not how to proceed, how to return, but I am calm and fearless and confident; if this reality were a dream, if I were asleep, what agonies had I suffered! When the Reason and the Will are away, what remains to us but Darkness and Dimness and a bewildering shame . . .[10]

Kant's tortuous account of the sense of the sublime in nature, when the awe-inspiring grandeur or violence about us makes us feel that we alone are superior to these forces, by virtue of our reason and our will – these thoughts are poured out in Coleridge's letter as if they were a spontaneous reaction to his predicament, as indeed, after his recent immersion in the philosophy of Kant, and his recent subjection to the irrationality and powerlessness induced by opium, they may almost have been.

Yet it is surely a very odd reaction. It seems to me that Kant was so much taken up with the supreme importance of providing a rational foundation for morality, so completely convinced that 'the moral law within' was the greatest possible source of the emotion of awe associated with sublimity in nature, that he mistook the real and obvious source of that emotion. It is not only simpler, but apparently nearer the truth to say that it is the vastness and power of nature, and her indifference to us that fills us with emotion in the contemplation of the untamed. It is not only that nature is not our possession: we are possessed or swallowed up by nature, an infinitely small element of that which surrounds us. Poor Coleridge, stuck on his ledge, might very well have been horrified by this very indifference, and we should have understood him better than we can sympathise with his use of his wild surroundings as a screen from which to

---

10 *Letters of Samuel Taylor Coleridge*, 6 volumes ed. E.L. Griggs (Clarendon Press, Oxford 1956–72) Vol. II.

read his own moral freedom. In the great chapters of the Book of Job where God speaks to His servant out of the whirlwind, and dwells on his ignorance of nature and helplessness in its face, it is the fact that wilderness exists, that the rain falls where no man is or has ever been that brings astonishment:

> Where wast thou when I laid the foundations of the earth? Declare if thou hast understanding . . . By what way is the light parted that scattered the east wind upon the earth? Who has divided a watercourse for the overflowing of waters or a way for the lightning of thunder; to cause it to rain on the wilderness, wherein there is no man; to satisfy the desolate and waste ground: and to cause the bud of the tender herb to spring forth? Hath the rain a father? Or who has begotten the drops of dew? . . . Canst thou bind the sweet influences of Pleiades, or loose the bands of Orion?[11]

Man is irrelevant to this vast conception of the natural world. (This whole passage, incidentally, is a superb example of literary genius crossing the line between stylistic and natural sublimity.)

It is in William Wordsworth, however, that we can trace most clearly the emergence of the romantic view of nature, as distinct, that is, from the picturesque. We can now begin to understand picturesque nature as essentially nature seen from an owner's point of view, as a painting may be owned; it is nature seen as a garden, even if the garden has already begun to be adorned with Gothic ruins and rustic tree stumps, rather than with Grecian temples and artificial lakes. It is nature manipulated.

Although the most complete analysis of his developing consciousness of the effects of nature on him as a poet is to be found in his great autobiographical poem, the *Prelude* (begun in 1798/99 and finished in draft in 1805, but often recast, and published posthumously in 1850), the poem that is perhaps most revealing of the new attitude towards nature is Lines Composed a Few Miles above Tintern Abbey on Revisiting the Banks of the Wye during a Tour July 13th 1798. The first of William Gilpin's *Travels in Search of the Picturesque* was concerned with the Wye Valley and South Wales, and was published in 1782 when Wordsworth was still a schoolboy. But, like everyone at the time, when he was a student, he would have fallen under Gilpin's influence; and the throwing off of this influence

---

[11] Job chapter 38 vv 28.

undoubtedly dictated both the choice of the location of the Lines, and a crucial part of their subject matter. For Gilpin, the view of Tintern Abbey was the high point of the Wye Tour, which contained an illustration of the Abbey itself, the compulsory central ruin in the middle distance, signifying the passage of time. He writes: 'The woods and glades intermixed; the winding of the river; the variety of the ground; the splendid ruin, contrasted with the objects of nature; and the elegant line formed by the summits of the hills, which include the whole; make all together a most inchanting piece of scenery'.

Wordsworth's lines, on the other hand, were written out of sight of the abbey, further upstream, and with no human artefact in sight, no distracting thoughts of the monks who once inhabited it: 'Once again / Do I behold these sleep and lofty cliffs, / Which on a wild secluded scene impress / Thoughts of more deep seclusion; and connect / The landscape with the quiet of the sky'. The thoughts of seclusion, the feeling of seclusion one might say, are impressed on the scene itself; that is what it, and the silence of the sky, wordlessly speaks. There is a passage in the eleventh book of the *Prelude*, entitled Imagination and Taste: How Impaired and Restored, that may be read as a gloss on this transition from the picturesque to the romantic. Wordsworth writes that there was a time when he took an 'unworthy' pleasure in nature; unworthy because he presumed to judge, classify and compare: 'disliking here, and there / Liking, by rules of mimic art transferr'd / To things above all art. But more – for this, . . . giving way / To a comparison of scene with scene, / Bent overmuch on superficial things, / Pampering myself with meagre novelties'. And he goes on to speak of the domination of the visual in such a superficial engagement with nature: 'I speak in recollection of a time / When the bodily eye, in every stage of life / The most despotic of our senses, gained / Such strength in me as often held my mind / In absolute dominion'. At this time, he writes, 'I roamed from hill to hill, from rock to rock, / Still craving combinations of new forms, / New pleasure, wider empire for the sight, / Proud of her own endowments, and rejoiced / To lay the inner faculties asleep'. The words in Tintern Abbey with which he describes his earlier visit to the Wye Valley echo those from the *Prelude*: 'when like a roe / I bounded o'er the mountains'. But now that he has returned, there is instead 'a sense sublime / Of something far more deeply interfused, / Whose dwelling is the light of setting suns, / And the round ocean and the living air, / And the blue sky, and in the mind of man, / A motion and a spirit, that impels / All thinking things, all objects of all thought, / And rolls through all things'.

Jonathan Bate[12] quotes this passage as illustrating Wordsworth's 'distinctive version of the Gaia Principle'. He explains:

> [Wordsworth] refuses to carve the world into object and subject; the same force animates both consciousness ('the mind of man') and 'all things'. Is a river or a plant the object of thought, or is it itself a thinking thing? Wordsworth says that it is both and that the distinction between subject and object is a murderous dissection.

I must postpone the consideration of the Gaia principle, a version of what has come to be known as 'spiritual ecology', until the next chapter. It is not clear to me that such a principle makes any sense. What is clear, however, is that, for Wordsworth, nature was not merely to be looked at, certainly not to be 'improved' or managed, but to be, in his words 'felt along the blood', succumbed to, as a source of deep reflection and sustenance. This is the romantic response to the natural world.

And already there is a paradox. Wilderness implies no people. The effect of the sublime demands solitude (or near-solitude). If we so wish we can keep other people out of our gardens, because we own them, but by what right can we presume to keep them away from that nature that we do not own, indeed whose very power over us lies in the fact that it is beyond ownership? If, like Wordsworth, we believe that responding to wild nature brings out the best in us, even causes us to be morally good, we should surely regard it as a positive duty to enable people other than ourselves to enjoy such responses for themselves. Yet, if we let them in to enjoy and profit from the sense of the sublime that we so highly value, that sense will inevitably be lost.

Moreover, if wild nature is not owned, and if we cannot even conceive of its being owned, who, if anyone, has responsibility for it? How is it possible that it should be prevented from being ruined or despoiled? The fact is that there is a contradiction in the idea of nature in the sense of wilderness being combined with human responsibility for its preservation. Bernard Williams, whose work I shall discuss in more detail below, put it thus: 'A natural park is not

---

12 Jonathan Bate, *The Song of the Earth* (Picador, London 2009) p.147.

nature but a park; a wilderness that is preserved is a definite, delimited, wilderness. The paradox is that we have to use our power to preserve a sense of what is not in our power. Anything that we leave untouched we have already touched'.[13] I shall return to this paradox in the final chapter.

Meanwhile, in noticing this paradox, we have reached the issue that will be explored in the remaining part of our investigation. It is the specific issue not of our enjoyment or exploitation of the natural world but of our responsibility for it. We have seen that ownership brings responsibility as well as enjoyment. We have seen that what we do not and cannot own brings a different kind of engagement with the natural world, which for those whose sensibility has been formed in part by the romantic movement is deeply valued, indeed may be regarded as the source of the most profound enjoyment of which human beings are capable. But we seem bent on destroying what we value; and the destruction seems not merely of something that gives aesthetic pleasure, however great, but of that which sustains us and all other life, and of which we are a part. We are not concerned only with 'the countryside' but with the whole planet, part of which is countryside, part towns and cities and urban sprawl, part oceans, part air. The question must be how we, all human beings, are to take responsibility for this. Before beginning to engage with this vast and daunting question, I want briefly to put aside two suggested answers.

It has often been suggested that we human beings must together take this responsibility, because we are 'stewards' charged by God to look after His creation. And in so far as stewards have responsibility for the management of things yet do not own those things, the concept of stewardship is apt enough. But a steward essentially has a master by whom he has been employed, and it is to this master that he is responsible for the care of his property. Moreover he is paid for his work, and it is therefore in his own immediate interest to carry it out well and with diligence. Neither of these things applies to the relation between human beings and that environment which they do not own, nature in the sense that we have been considering it. If we have a duty of care, it must be one that we ourselves have

[13] Bernard Williams, 'Must a concern for the environment be centred on human beings?', *Making Sense of Humanity* (Cambridge University Press, Cambridge 1995) pp. 233ff.

voluntarily imposed upon ourselves. We receive no immediate or obvious reward for carrying it out; indeed it may involve considerable sacrifice and expense. To say that we are stewards of the natural world can be no more than to make use of a metaphor, derived from the analogy already noticed, that a steward looks after what he does not own; it is a natural metaphor, no doubt, but hardly illuminating, still less motivating, except for those with a very literal understanding of the Judaeo-Christian tradition and the relation between God the creator and His creatures. For a steward is answerable to his employer; we no longer seem to be answerable to anyone, if we are indifferent to the world in which we live.

There is another suggestion that seeks to motivate us to take responsibility for the global environment. It is sometimes asserted that we hold the whole of nature in trust for future generations, and that it is therefore our duty as trustees to ensure that nature is managed in their interests, not our own. Apart from a doubt about whether it is for the sake only of future human beings that we should care for our environment, to which I shall return in due course, the drawback of this way of thinking is, manifestly, the same as that of talking about stewardship. We may if we choose think of our position with regard to future people as analogous to that of trustees. But no trust has been, or ever could be, set up. Once again we are dealing in metaphor. Yet what is needed if the environment, that is the air, water and earth, is to be protected from harm, is practical policy; and no viable policy can be founded on a metaphor, however natural and superficially intelligible.

The question of our global responsibility thus remains to be addressed.

7. Taking responsibility for the planet

There exists one enormous part of the planet which is owned by nobody, which is almost totally wilderness and yet for which those who work in it and care for it take complete joint responsibility. This is Antarctica, the largest continent in the world, which contains within it more than 70 per cent of all the fresh water that there is. It is a vast natural laboratory, where 28 different countries are working side by side in more than 40 research stations; some nations have made territorial claims, but none of these has been recognised. This is in accordance with the Antarctic Treaty, under whose terms the different countries work, and which the UK was the first to ratify in 1961. An updated treaty has recently been ratified. This treaty has been described as international law at its best. Under the terms of the treaty, anyone leaving Chile, from which Antarctica is reached, is briefed that they must take nothing out of the continent when they leave, and they must leave nothing behind. Absolutely all waste material, including sewage and food waste, must be put in bags, frozen and sent back to Chile. Speaking in the House of Lords in support of the updated treaty, Lord Forsyth of Drumlean told the House of his expedition two years earlier to climb Mount Vinson, in the interior, where it is so cold that no animals, not even bacteria, can survive. 'It is a completely lifeless place', he said:

> For me, it was a quite astonishing, almost spiritual, experience. If you stand on a mountain in Antarctica on a calm day . . . the air is so clear and unpolluted you can see for many more miles than we are used to doing in other parts of the globe. The thing that is most striking is the silence. There are no birds or aeroplanes. You look out on a completely unspoiled environment.[1]

---

[1] House of Lords, Hansard, 1 February 2013, col. 1773.

This cannot be said of other remote mountains of the world, including Everest and Kilimanjaro, which are now littered with rubbish, on all the routes to the top and back, and seriously polluted by the growing number of tourist mountaineers.

And now even Antarctica is under threat, in that there is an increasing number of tourists in those months of the year when there is daylight; this was indeed the reason why the treaty needed to be updated, so that insurance arrangements could be agreed, to deal with any catastrophes, such as oil spills or the break-up of ships, that might pollute the seas. *The Times* of 30 January 2014 carried a full-page advertisement, offering exclusively to its readers a cut-price tour to Antarctica via South America, praising in particular the 'sparkling glaciers', the long hours of daylight in which to enjoy the 'breathtaking scenery and abundant wildlife' combined with the on-board shopping and other amenities of the cruise vessel.

I do not suggest, of course, that other areas of solitude and wilderness can be kept as pure as the Antarctic, or treated with as much reverence and respect. I want to point only to the success of international law in just one place. And even here one must cautiously add 'so far'. For it is not only intrepid (and, it has to be said, often frivolously motivated) tourists who pose a threat. As an effect of global warming, scientists working in Antarctica have begun to be able to dig to reveal rich seams of minerals, and there is evidence of oil. It may not be long before, despite the international treaty, pressure will mount for territorial claims to be recognised so that these vast resources may be exploited, as has already happened in the Arctic. There is also increasing fishing in the seas, with all the attendant risks of pollution, overfishing and an altered ecology.

So it may be that the Antarctic Treaty system is not as secure as one would hope, and the clarity and vast silence of the continent will not last. It is, after all, a special case: the reason why it remains unspoiled by human beings is not only that it is so harsh an environment, so very unfriendly to life, but that all those who work there are devoted to a single object, scientific research. In this it is like a great university, with many scientific departments, not in competition with each other but pursuing the same ends side by side, and motivated as far as possible to conserve an environment that enables these ends to be pursued. This makes it extraordinarily unlike the rest of the world, in which territorial claims, competing interests, population growth and consequent poverty and the pollution of the environment by carbon emissions seem inevitably and insatiably to prevail.

It may be the case that population growth and even greenhouse gases are not dangers for Antarctica; but the real possibility of overfishing provides a good example of what is now widely known as 'The Tragedy of the Commons'. This name derives from an influential article under that title, by an American scientist, Garrett Hardin, written as long ago as 1968, though frequently updated and republished thereafter.[2] According to his argument, overpopulation is the single cause of the inevitable self-destruction by human beings of their world. He is extremely ruthless in his proposed solutions, including legislation to prohibit families of more than one child; but we need not follow him down that route. The reason why overpopulation will destroy the world, he argues, is that when land is privately owned, it is conserved, and its exploitation carefully controlled so that its utility may be sustainable; but when it is held in common, each individual will take as much from it as he can until its resources are entirely used up. For instance, if there is common land on which herdsmen may all graze their cattle, the rational herdsman will calculate that it will not make a lot of difference if he adds one more animal to his flock. And then another and another. And all the herdsmen will make the same calculation, there being no individual person to take the responsibility of planned conservation:

> Each man is locked into a system that compels him to increase his herd without limit – in a world that is limited. Ruin is the destination to which all men rush, each man pursuing his own best interest in a society that believes in the freedom of the commons. Freedom of a commons brings ruin to all.[3]

Hardin argues that there is no scientific or technical solution to this problem. A change of moral attitudes must be sought.

Turning specifically to overfishing, he says 'Maritime nations still respond automatically to the shibboleth of "the freedom of the seas". Professing to believe in the "inexhaustible resources of the oceans", they bring species after species of fish and whales closer to extinction'. We are less complacent, perhaps, than we were in 1968

---

[2] Garrett Hardin, 'The Tragedy of the Commons' (1968) New Series 162 (3859) *Science* 1243–8.

[3] Ibid., p. 1244.

about the dangers of overfishing and the complex ecology involved. But the point remains. For Hardin recognises that while land can be parcelled out by enclosure, so that individuals can own different bits of land, it is difficult to enforce legal ownership of different areas of the high seas.

The word 'tragedy' is used for the ruin that Hardin foresees in the strict literary sense: there is an inevitable disastrous outcome which the protagonists walk into blindly, but which we, or rather the scientists standing by as the audience, know must happen. This is 'Tragic Irony'.

Thirty years after Hardin's article was published, it was re-examined in another article which appeared in the same periodical,[4] in which the authors rightly criticised Hardin for suggesting that the only alternatives to common land and 'the freedom of the seas' were either central state control of all such unowned areas, or private ownership of different parts of the commons, that is, 'either socialism or the privatism of free enterprise', to quote Hardin's words. The authors argue, on the contrary, that there have long been successful mechanisms for joint ownership of common pool resources (CPRs), (some of which were considered in chapter 5 above); and that on a relatively small scale this is the way we should go, in order to avoid the destruction of the environment. They produce evidence derived from aerial photography in Nepal to suggest that what works best as a means of conserving the environment is a set of rules governing access to and use of the resource, which has been drawn up locally, and locally enforced and monitored. And this is very plausible. But they admit that, when we come to consider global resources, what they call 'Global Commons'[5] there will be a need for complex international treaties of an unprecedented kind. But, increasingly, since the publication of this article, we have to raise the question whether it is possible to agree such treaties.

It is not that attempts have not been made to reach international agreement on the action that needs to be taken. In 1997 the Kyoto Protocol was set up which established a central target for emissions among industrialised nations. But the USA did not join in,

---

4 E. Ostrom, J. Burger, C.B. Field, R.B. Norgaard and D. Policansky, 'Revisiting the commons, local lessons, global challenges' (9 April 1999) New Series 284 (5412) *Science* 278–82.

5 Ibid., p. 281.

and since then Russia, Canada and Japan have all pulled out. It has not worked; nor was agreement reached in 2012 at the Copenhagen climate summit. That held in Warsaw in November 2013 also ended in acrimony. Those poorer countries most affected by natural disasters such as typhoon Hayan, which devastated the Philippines earlier in the same month, walked out en bloc. Connecting the increased prevalence and intensity of such extreme events with global warming brought about by pollution (a connection for which there is increasing scientific evidence), they demanded that a new mechanism be set up, under which richer countries automatically paid 'loss and damage' compensation to poorer countries when such a disaster occurred. The European Union (EU), USA, Australia and other developed countries understandably regard this as an impossibly high price to pay, and a price that is open-ended and unpredictable. For one thing, no scientist can predict the speed of the global warming that is currently taking place. There are those who, in any case, argue that global warming will be positively beneficial for at least another sixty years, and that human beings will gradually adapt to it. But, that aside, though the EU, for example, is budgeting €180 billion to be spent on combating climate change between 2014 and 2020, this will mostly be spent on domestic policies, such as developing new methods of agriculture, and energy saving, rather than on any redistribution of finance, such as the poorer countries demand.

The difficulty of establishing an international treaty that every country will ratify is easy to understand: there is a conflict of interests for every individual nation. On the one hand it must meet the cost of its own economic growth and environmental improvement, and on the other, vast sums of money are demanded to help those countries whose atmosphere is most choked with pollution and whose land is most severely wasted by the destruction of grasslands, by floods and the erosion of the coast. To agree to a policy of international aid on such a scale would amount to a genuine redistribution of income, worldwide; such a policy is never likely to be popular in the countries whose wealth is thereby going to diminish. This conflict is especially sharp as each country must concentrate on recovering from recession and on investing all it can afford in competitive development. It is no wonder that the warnings of scientists are neglected or denied credibility by those who have actually to make policy. The louder the scientists' voices, the more their opponents will point to past warnings of disasters that have never been fulfilled. But even those who believe what the climate experts tell them cannot agree. Meanwhile the pollution, not only of the atmosphere but also of the land and sea, continues.

So what do we really want for the spoiled world that is not Antarctica? What each one wants for that tiny part of the world that he owns we can probably quite easily say: we do not necessarily want to preserve it for ever the same. We may want carefully to improve it, and make the best imaginable use of its potentialities and products. But above all we want not to harm it, either by neglect or deliberate actions, our own or those of such other people as we let loose on it. And this, I believe, is not necessarily because we want to hand it down in good shape to our heirs. We may have no heirs, or may know well that if they exist they will have no use for what is ours. The protectiveness and the deep pleasure (by which I mean pleasure for which nothing is a substitute, but which is uniquely valued) that we take in what we own seems to me, in fact, to be more akin to love than to any other emotion, love, that is, for the thing itself, and the relation in which it stands to ourselves, and we to it.

To some extent I believe that this sort of love, this combination of protectiveness and pleasure, is increasingly acknowledged as something that may be felt towards our wider environment, as well as to that fragment of it that we own. Such feeling is reinforced, in the context of the planet as a whole, by a sense of amazement at the variety and complexity of the living world, and an increased understanding of the interdependence of one part with another, both within individual organisms and within the vast system as a whole. As long ago as 1971, a consultative committee was set up by the United Nations to produce a report on the human environment. This report was written by the economist, Barbara Ward, with the secretary of the commission, René Dubos, and published the next year.[6] The emphasis of the report was on the unity of the planet, and the final chapter is an impassioned plea for joint action by all nations, not just the developed nations, to bring to an end the destruction of the planet, through pollution. For, the authors argued, it is pollution, in all its forms, which will eventually lead to the disappearance of life on earth. The action needed, it is claimed,

6 Barbara Ward and René Dubos, *Only One Earth: The Care and Maintenance of a Small Planet* (Penguin, Harmondsworth 1972).

is worldwide education, and a radical redistribution of resources. A comparison is drawn with the crisis that faced the internal economy of nations after the Industrial Revolution, when the gap between rich and poor had to be narrowed, if a breakdown of society, 'into revolt and anarchy', was to be avoided, and this was done through education and new social policies, funded by new forms of taxation. The book ends with the optimistic assertion that people are beginning to feel a new loyalty, and a 'new vision of where man belongs in his final security and his final sense of dignity and identity'.[7]

Forty years on, the emergence of any such new vision may seem as far off as ever. We know more about pollution and climate change than we did, and legislation, both within individual states and to a certain extent across borders has proliferated. Yet the insatiability of human greed, human poverty and the apparent impossibility of enforcing international law still militate against any such concerted action as the report called for. And, as I have already suggested, it is difficult for the government of any country to justify a redistribution of resources at the expense of its own economic recovery and continuing prosperity. Democratic governments, in framing their policies, are expected to make broadly utilitarian judgements about the wellbeing of the people whom they govern. And that means people who exist now and who will exist in a relatively foreseeable future, as citizens of one individual nation.

Nevertheless, I think we may perhaps detect a growing sense that it is not the protection solely of the human future that is the concern of environmentalists. In the UK, the Environmental Protection Act (1990), though directed primarily to combat the harmful, or offensive, effects on human beings of pollution of the environment (air, water and earth) yet recognised the concept of harm to the environment itself as an interrelated ecological system within which human beings, but not they alone, live their lives. This was in fact a revolutionary idea in legislation. It had been taken for granted until then that, though the environment might be spoiled, and in this sense harmed, it was harm to the human beings whose environment it was that was to be prevented by legislation.

In the same year that Barbara Ward's report was published there appeared an article in the *Southern California Law Review* by

---

[7] Ibid., p. 296.

Professor Christopher Stone, entitled 'Should trees have standing? Toward legal rights for natural objects'.[8] In the preface to the 2012 reprint of the article, Professor Philippe Sands points to the changes that have taken place since 1972:

> Let us not forget that in the world of 1972 there were no rules of European Community environmental law; not a single textbook on public international law had a chapter on the environment; and the only country to have an Environmental Protection Agency (or its equivalent) was the United States.[9]

Stone's article raised the possibility of putting natural objects, including animals other than human beings as well as living organisms such as trees, virtually on a level of legal equality with human beings, plaintiffs to be represented in court by a guardian or next friend to defend their interests, as human infants or incompetent persons may be represented. He took as one central example the case of *Sierra Club v Hickely*.[10] I quote what I wrote about the case in commenting on Stone's argument:

> The US Forest Service had granted permission for a commercial company, Walt Disney Enterprises Inc., to develop a wilderness Valley in the Sierra Nevada mountains in California, the Mineral Springs Park. The proposal was to build a vast complex of hotels, restaurants and other amenities, making appropriate roads for access. The Sierra Club applied for standing to bring a civil case against the company, but this was not allowed. The Ninth Court of Appeal ruled not because they thought the Forest Service had been right to permit the development, but on the grounds that the club did not satisfy the criteria for standing. 'After all', they ruled, 'the Club does not allege that it is "aggrieved" or "adversely affected"'. Stone argued, on the contrary that even if it were true that the injury to the Sierra Club was tenuous, the injury to the Mineral King, the park itself, was not. 'If standing were the barrier, why not designate Mineral King, the wilderness area, as plaintiff adversely affected, let the Sierra Cub be designated the guardian or attorney, and get on with the merits'. The real issue, he argued, was not what all the digging out of roads would do to members of the club, but what it would do to the valley. 'Why not come right out and say that?'[11]

---

8 Reprinted with commentaries in *Journal of Human Rights and the Environment* vol. 3 (2012) Edward Elgar Journals.

9 Ibid., p. 3.

10 Ibid., nl xiii.

11 Ibid., p. 57.

Stone opined that to bring about such a change, radical though it might seem, would not in fact be too difficult. And it would, he suggested, go a long way towards remedying the unduly anthropocentric view we tend to take of environmental problems.

In what I wrote in 2012, I argued, and still maintain, first, that our environmental laws, at any rate both in the UK, the rest of Europe and the USA, already allow us to place a natural object, such as a tree, under a protection order, prohibiting its destruction; secondly, that it is absurd to suggest that we can look at things 'from the point of view of natural objects' including wilderness valleys. Although I have argued above (Chapter 3) that we may speak of the interests of my lawn, referring to that kind of treatment that would allow it to flourish, I believe that there can be no such thing as 'the point of view' of a natural non-human object, animal, vegetable or mineral. We human beings and we alone have 'points of view'. And this is because we alone can take stock of and articulate where we stand, and what we see from that standpoint when we contemplate nature as a whole and our relations with it. We, and we alone, have imagination. This means that we alone can think about things that are not actually at a particular moment in front of our eyes, and can use language to articulate these thoughts. It is this that gives us our anthropocentric 'point of view', and to that extent we are stuck with it.

All the same, it must be said that, forty years on, *The Times* for 3rd December 2013 carried the story of four chimpanzees, who lived in New York State, filing a suit to be heard at the New York Supreme Court, claiming wrongful imprisonment, and demanding that they be released into a reserve where their needs could be properly met. Their advocates, appearing in Court to plead on their behalf, were an organisation known as The Non-human Rights Project, made up of lawyers and primatologists, but which may also contain botanists, for all I know, to look after the rights of trees. At any rate Stone must certainly regard this as a step in the right direction.

For, though we may not be able completely to shake off our anthropocentric point of view, we can seek to modify our attitudes, and such a modification has, I believe, slowly been taking place in the last forty years, since the 1970s. The gradual change is coming about, I suggest, through a development in our understanding of the idea of 'values', a word seldom used by philosophers, and indeed regarded by them with deep suspicion, at least in the mid-century, but now reinstated. For after the brief flourishing of Logical Positivism, introduced to the English-speaking world in 1936 by A.J. Ayer,[12] the absolute dichotomy between verifiable fact and value, which characterised that movement, lingered on in the fields of ethics and aesthetics, and values were not thought worth discussing directly, because, according to positivist dogma, what was held to be valuable was a matter of taste, fashion or propaganda, and had nothing to do with scientific understanding of the world. Value judgements when contrasted with statements of scientific fact were strictly meaningless. For to be meaningful, according to the positivists of the so-called Vienna Circle, a proposition must be verifiable by observation. Such was the dogma set out in Ayer's *Language, Truth and Logic* with all the fervour of a convert. If any verifiable facts were to be ascertained about values, these would be statistical facts, discovered by opinion polls, and reflecting what people said they valued at any given time. They could, of course, say what they liked, but what they said would be meaningless because unverifiable, as far as the scientific facts were concerned.

The positivists' narrow concept of meaning did not survive the Second World War, though the dichotomy of evaluative and descriptive meaning lingered on, as I have said, in the fields of ethics and aesthetics for some time (and is still to be found in the writings of some of those who studied philosophy as undergraduates just after the war, and have not studied it since).

Now, however, it is widely taken to be a fact that some things are valued by all animals, including human beings, and are things that are sought by them, their opposites shunned. There are some values, however, that are peculiar to human beings. It follows that, among human language-users, an enormous number of the words that we use to talk about the world are both descriptive and evaluative; the two aspects cannot be separated. A word descriptive of something nasty (say, 'slimy') conveys both the way the thing is, and our attitude towards it. To describe someone as 'dumpy' cannot be construed as a compliment, nor even as neutral; and 'noisy' at least when used of music, children or traffic, is generally a bad word, as much evaluative as descriptive.

The concept of a value, in the case of any animal, is closely related to that of a need, and also to that of pleasure and pain. Thus the

---

[12] A.J. Ayer, *Language, Truth and Logic* (Macmillan, London 1936).

recognition of shared objectively ascertainable values is in part due to the spread of the legal concept of human rights. There being no preordained list of human rights, in order to succeed in a case for breach of human rights, one must rely on a general consensual understanding of what no human being ought to inflict on another, such as torture, arbitrary imprisonment, expulsion from a domicile, starvation, the wrongful seizure of property and so on. If someone says of a country that it has a 'shocking human rights record', we all understand the kind of thing that goes on in that country. So if there is growing agreement about what 'human rights' are, then this is tantamount to an agreement about human values. (And those who claim that animals other than human beings have rights may, if they wish, define animal rights and values in terms of those things which various animals need if they are to flourish, and of which they ought not to be deprived. Such is the basis of the case for the New York State chimpanzees.) But this needs-related concept of value seems unduly narrow to cover the things that specifically human animals value. 'Man cannot live by bread alone'; he has, as I have said, the power to think about the way things are in general, and to aspire to make them better, or at least not worse; to love and embrace some aspects of the world as he sees it in his imagination, and to hate others, and these are his intrinsic values, conceived as valuable without direct reference to those basic needs (for nutrition, hydration or shelter) that he shares with other animals. For most human beings, for example, though not for other animals, justice itself is one of the highest values. It is perhaps in pursuit of some such intrinsic value that environmentalists urge us to take responsibility for saving the planet, treating it as our own, rather as we may be asked to give money to restore a painting that is degenerating, or a fine building that is on the verge of collapse.

In 1974 the Australian philosopher, John Passmore, published a book entitled *Man's Responsibility for the Environment*.[13] He was in no doubt that human beings and their activities were the major cause of all environmental ills; and he argued that therefore human beings must take on responsibility for the remedy of those ills. In fact it could be argued that there is no necessary connection between those

---

[13] John Passmore, *Man's Responsibility for the Environment* (Duckworth, London 1974).

two propositions; one might say that even if it is human activity that hastens or exacerbates climate change through the use of fossil fuels, or causes the extinction of species of fish through its fishing policies, these are matters of economic necessity more pressing than any consideration of what may happen on earth in the distant future. Moreover it is possible that human beings have already caused irreversible damage, as many prophets of doom suggest. To require them to be responsible for changing the future would be like requiring someone who had developed terminal lung cancer by smoking to be responsible for his own treatment. But at any rate Passmore held that the actions of human beings had laid on them the obligation to put things right, and his question was how it is to be done.

In his book, Passmore offered no specific recipe for what such a remedy might be: only further and more determined scientific research could discover it, and the outcome of research can obviously never be predicted. But in general he proposed that human beings must abandon the proprietorial attitude to nature that he believed they still adopted, behaving 'as if they owned it', and could use it as they pleased; instead they should act as stewards. (But see above, chapter 4.) He also argued for better education of the general public. This has to some extent come about since he wrote. There is a far greater awareness of damage to the environment than there was forty years ago; and there is also, as I have suggested, a greater awareness of the infinite richness and variety of the natural world, which itself induces love and astonishment and a desire to avoid its harm. This feeling for nature has been greatly increased by the technical marvels of photography, and the consequent popularity of natural world programmes on prime-time television.

However, to turn this feeling, even if it is growing, into motivation strong enough to produce policies that would entail immediate sacrifices would also involve our putting our trust in scientists when they produce evidence of what is happening and how things might be changed. Such trust has not proved easy to bring about in the intervening forty years. And even if we believe the most doom-laden of the scientific messages, there is still a gap between our motives for continuing to live as we do, and incurring the expense and perceived deprivation of changing our ways. Are we really being asked to give up our refrigerators, cars and food imported by air from abroad?

Passmore was exceptionally scornful of those who try to motivate us to action by religious or quasi-religious rhetoric, what has come to be called 'spiritual environmentalism', or 'spiritual ecology'. He is right, in that, though believers may derive their own sense of global responsibility from their religious beliefs, the framing of policy and the enforcement of law must be based on arguments that will appeal to non-believers. This is a perfectly general truth. It is of no use to attempt to frame abortion law, for example, in terms of a belief that human life must be protected from the moment of conception because life is a gift from God. This belief is indeed the foundation of anti-abortion policy for those who hold it; but for those who do not, it is powerless to move them. It is remarkable how long it has taken for people to grasp the manifest fact that arguments based on religion appeal only to the religious.

We have already noted the emptiness of the metaphor of stewardship for those who do not believe in a creator God (and it may seem odd that Passmore should have relied on it; but, though hostile to religion, he acknowledged the strength of the Judaeo-Christian tradition in Western society, and thus the ready intelligibility of the metaphor). At any rate, policy-making must be independent of religion, and if it is to be implemented, must rely on something other than religious belief.

It is not only traditional Judaeo-Christian religion that is called in aid of care for the environment. Bhuddism, though worshipping no god, has always held the universe and all life within it to be sacred; and recently there has arisen the quasi-religion of the Gaia hypothesis, already mentioned in chapter 6. This is the brain-child of a physicist, James Lovelock, who, though he worked during his long life for many different organisations, including NASA, investigating conditions for possible life on other planets, was mainly an independent scientist. He records that the hypothesis (or principle or theory) came to him as a kind of revelation, when he was looking at photographs of the earth taken from space, as it was seen by the astronauts on the Apollo mission. He saw the planet, he says, as a single living organism.[14] The whole planet, he says, is a complex system, all of whose component parts work together interdependently to maintain the conditions necessary for life. It will

---

14 James Lovelock, *Gaia: A New Look at Life on Earth* (Oxford University Press, Oxford 1979).

continuously produce an equilibrium between its components, none favoured above any other. It is the unity of the planet that is at the centre of the hypothesis (as it was in the earlier report by Barbara Ward, cited, above). Although Lovelock records that the realisation of unity came to him as a kind of epiphany, a moment of truth, he insists that it is in fact a scientific theory, for which evidence can be found. It is therefore perhaps a pity that he adopted the suggestion of his one-time neighbour, the powerfully imaginative novelist, William Golding, to call the theory Gaia. For Gaia is undoubtedly the name of a goddess, and it is the vaguely spiritual aspect of the hypothesis that has been most appealing to those who are inclined to adopt it, and which it is hoped will provide motivation for human restraint in exploiting the environment. The goddess-like properties of the planet are reinforced by the title of Lovelock's more recent book, *The Revenge of Gaia.*[15] Surely it is gods and goddesses who can wreak vengeance, not organically unified planets? Once again we seem to be offered what is either a metaphor or an implied theology.

We saw in chapter 6 that Jonathan Bate ascribed to Wordsworth a 'distinctive version of the Gaia principle', which he found especially in the lines which end 'A motion and a spirit, that impels / All thinking things, all objects of all thought, / And rolls through all things'. If these lines imply any distinctive version of a theory, it seems to me to approximate more closely to a once popular theory of the nature of the universe published somewhat earlier than Lovelock's, now I believe wholly forgotten. This was the theory, like Lovelock's offered as evidence-based and scientific, contained in Teilhard de Chardin's *The Phenomenon of Man.*[16] Admittedly this theory was supposed to show that the moving force of everything in the universe was evolution, a concept of which Wordsworth knew nothing. But the idea of evolution appealed to is itself peculiar, involving the notion that if something has emerged in one creature, it must already have been in existence in every other creature in which it will eventually emerge. So, as human beings have an inner as well as an outer life, that is to say they possess consciousness, it must follow that every other thing in the world also possesses this feature, if only in a rudimentary,

---

15 James Lovelock, *The Revenge of Gaia* (Basic Books, New York 2006).

16 Pierre Teilhard de Chardin *Le Phénomène humain* (Éditions de Seuil, Paris 1955); Bernard Wall (tr.), *The Phenomenon of Man* (Harper, New York 1959) with intro. by Julian Huxley.

latent form. Given this evolutionary axiom, de Chardin wrote: 'we are logically forced to assume . . . the existence of some sort of psyche in every corpuscle' and 'by the very fact of the individualization of our planet, a certain mass of elementary consciousness was originally imprisoned in the matter of earth'. Everything thinks. This manifest (and deliberately obscure) gobbledegook was embraced with astonishing enthusiasm. The book was a best seller. I suppose people like to feel that things are too profound for them to understand. It was partly so popular because it was endorsed by the biologist and broadcaster, Julian Huxley, who wrote an introduction to the English translation. I remember in the 1960s sitting next to him at lunch (we were fellow governors of a school founded by his mother, at which both he and I were ex-pupils) and being told what a wonderful theory this was, and how it would make people take seriously the damage to the earth caused by chemical fertilisers, the then most apparently serious environmental threat.

However not all scientists were so much impressed; and Sir Peter Medawar, a far more serious biologist than Huxley, wrote an excoriating article, exposing the fraudulence of the scientific claims of *The Phenomenon of Man*. He ends with these words:

> I have read and studied *The Phenomenon of Man* with real distress, even with despair. Instead of wringing our hands over the Human Predicament, we should attend to those parts of it which are wholly remediable, above all to the gullibility which makes it possible for people to be taken in by such a bag of tricks as this. If it were an innocent, passive gullibility, it would be excusable; but all too clearly, alas, it is an active willingness to be deceived.[17]

The particular kind of nonsense that went to make up *The Phenomenon of Man* may have gone away, but it is true that all too many people like to read things about the planet as a whole and their place within it that they do not understand, deriving positive satisfaction from the unintelligibility and supposed profundity of the propositions presented to them. But the two theories we have considered in this chapter, both proposing a homogeneity within the planet as a whole, human and non-human alike, are instances, albeit dubiously intelligible and certainly not evidence-based, of a great

---

[17] Peter Medawar, *The Phenemenon of Man* (reprinted in *Pluto's Republic*, Oxford University Press, Oxford 1982).

revolution in thought that occurred in the mid-twentieth century, and is now part of the normal assumptions of philosophers, psychologists, environmentalists and others who think about the way things are. The revolution consists in the almost total rejection of Cartesian dualism, the expulsion of the Ghost from the Machine, to use the words, not coined, but brilliantly exploited by Gilbert Ryle, whose major work, *The Concept of Mind*[18] was part of the revolution. I have said something about Cartesian dualism in chapter 1 but now it is time to examine it and its demise a bit more closely.

Dualism is the belief that mind, or consciousness, and matter are two completely different things. The true origins of its demise lie in Germany in the period before the Second World War, with a group of philosophers known as phenomenologists, and especially with Franz Brentano and his pupil, Edmund Husserl. Although Husserl adopted a kind of Cartesian introspective method in an attempt to examine the nature of the content of consciousness itself, stripping it as far as possible of everyday assumptions and associations ('putting the world in brackets') he differed from Descartes (as well as from Descartes' successors) in finding no experience in his consciousness that did not speak directly of an external world. It was the intrinsic nature of consciousness to be 'intensional', the word Brentano had used to mean 'to be directed towards something', or to be 'of' something. There are not three things to be related, as Descartes believed, namely 'I' the thinking being, my *pensé* or idea, and a possible cause of this in the world, but only two, me, a conscious physical object, and another physical object in the world. The question 'how is the material world related to what is in my mind?' ceases to be problematic. Towards the end of his life, Husserl's phenomenology became more and more arcane, and, to me at least, less and less intelligible or interesting.

But the reaction of two French philosophers, Maurice Merleau-Ponty and Jean-Paul Sartre illustrates the impression that Husserl's phenomenology made. Sartre went to Germany in 1939 to study his work, and wrote a short article as soon as he got back, which was published in the *Nouvelle Revue Française*. He was clearly in a state of high excitement; he had discovered a philosophy that was in revolt against what he called the 'digestive' view of perception according to which

---

[18] Gilbert Ryle, *The Concept of Mind* (Hutchinson, London 1949).

> [An object was] sucked into the consciousness of its beholder to become a mental entity, an idea or an impression. Husserl persistently affirms that you cannot dissolve things in consciousness. You see this tree to be sure. But you see it just where it is: at the side of the road, in the midst of the dust, alone and writhing in the heat, eight miles from the Mediterranean. It could not enter your consciousness.

Material things do not change their nature and become mental things in being perceived. They are revealed to us as they are, and not only in their tangible, visible, audible aspects, but as lovable, hateful, terrifying:

> We are delivered from the 'internal life' . . . since everything is finally outside, everything, even ourselves. Outside, in the world among others. It is not in some hiding place that we shall find ourselves; it is outside, on the road, in the town, in the midst of the crowd, a thing among things, a man among men.[19]

Meanwhile, Merleau-Ponty was working on his book, *The Phenomenology of Perception* which was quite explicitly designed to expound Husserl's philosophy in French.[20] He too insisted that the crucial point of Husserl's revolution was his elimination of the 'inner world' as mediating between human beings and the spatial environment in which they lived. Instead, he regarded human beings as essentially physical objects among others. And one must not underestimate the genuinely revolutionary nature, for a French philosopher, of overthrowing the Cartesianism on which his philosophical education had been founded. It was throwing away his Bible.

Gilbert Ryle said of his own book, *The Concept of Mind*, that, though he knew it would be taken to be an expression of crude behaviourism, in fact it would be better read as an essay in phenomenology, thus acknowledging his debt to Husserl, whom few other English-speaking philosophers had read. However, it is neither to Husserl nor to Ryle that the anti-Cartesian revolution is generally ascribed, but to Ludwig Wittgenstein, not one prone to admit to having read the works of other philosophers, let alone to having been influenced by them. And it is probably right to credit him with

---

[19] Reprinted, Joseph P. Fell (tr.) (1970) 1(2) *Journal of the British Society of Phenomenology* 4–50.

[20] Maurice Merleau-Ponty, *The Phenomenology of Perception* (Gallimard, Paris 1945).

the widespread change in our way of thinking about the relation between human beings and the world they inhabit. For he thought of human beings, not so much as things among things as men among men, essentially language-users and communicators; and it was from his insight into the nature of language and the games we can play with it that his anti-Cartesianism flowed.

In the year 1948, as a final-year undergraduate, I had spent a vast amount of time writing essays about the Problem of Perception, starting with the works of Descartes, and ending with those of Bertrand Russell and A.J. Ayer. I was being unofficially (and much to my terror) taught at the time by Elizabeth Anscombe, who was engaged on the compilation and translation of Wittgenstein's *Philosophical Investigations*. She used sometimes to show me sections of her translation, for me to comment on her version, though my German was not very good. I remember being completely bowled over by one passage she gave me. I felt that I had been let into an enormous and profound secret: no one had read this except Elizabeth and, I suppose, some of her friends and pupils. An air of total mystery hung around Wittgenstein. Even those who had attended the seminars he had given in Cambridge were frequently expelled as traitors, plagiarists or misrepresenters of the true gospel. Elizabeth Anscombe, however, was a favoured and trusted disciple, who, I thought, must hold the key to the mystery. Wittgenstein had visited Oxford the year before and held two baffling meetings, of which I could remember little but the aura of genius that had surrounded him, the long periods of total silence as he sat clutching his furrowed brow, and the extreme rudeness to him of a retired philosopher, famous in his day for plainness of speech and a precision of expression. But I did record in my diary one thing that Wittgenstein said, in response to the paper read to the meeting on 'cogito ergo sum'. He said, 'If a man looking at the sun said "I think it's going to rain, therefore I am", I should not understand him'. This was a hint of how he thought about the way language worked or failed to work.

The passage that so much struck me starts at paragraph 293 (p. 100 of Anscombe's translation):[21]

---

[21] Ludwig Wittgenstein, *Philosophical Investigations*, G.E.M. Anscombe (tr.) (Blackwell, Oxford 1968).

> Suppose everyone had a box with something in it: we call it a 'beetle'. No one can look into anyone else's box, and everyone says he knows what a beetle is only by looking at his beetle. Here it would be quite possible for everyone to have something different in his box. One might even imagine the thing constantly changing. But suppose the word 'beetle' had a use in these people's language? If so it would not be used as the name of a thing. The thing in the box has no place in the language-game at all, not even as a something; for the box might even be empty. – No, one can 'divide through' by the thing in the box; it cancels out, whatever it is. That is to say, if we construe the grammar of the expression of sensation on the model of 'object and its designation' the object drops out of consideration as irrelevant . . . If you admit that you haven't any notion what kind of thing it might be that he has before him, what leads you into saying, in spite of that, that he has something before him? Isn't it as if I were to say of someone 'he has something. But I don't know whether it is money or debts or an empty till'.

This was unlike anything I had read before. I had never heard of Husserl or Sartre (except as a playwright); Gilbert Ryle's book had not yet been published. I had been to J.L. Austin's amazingly funny lectures[22] on Ayer's theory of perception through the medium of 'sense data' (but it was Austin on Aristotle that had most excited me). In Wittgenstein's beetle passage there seemed to be encapsulated a new understanding that language was not first given meaning by private inner experiences, and then somehow translated into the public domain, but was first and foremost, and essentially about shared things, things common to me and others, and therefore necessarily things in the world. 'Finally everything is outside.' And this is what language is about. It was a genuine revolution in the concept of language and thus of the place of language-users in the world.

I entirely share the current assumption that these anti-dualistic ideas, whatever their origin, have by now come to permeate the thinking not just of philosophers, but of critics and writers, including environmentalists as well. We no longer think of ourselves as separated from the external world by the ghostly ideas or sensations that constitute our inner life and haunt our material bodies (though children still ask, as they always have, 'How do I know that when I see something green I see the same as what you see when you see something green?'). We are our spatial and material bodies and

[22] Published posthumously: J.L. Austin, *Sense and Sensibilia*, G.J. Warnock (ed.) (Oxford University Press, Oxford 1963).

belong among other such bodies. This shift in thinking about the inner and the outer may well indirectly affect our thinking about our environment, and even about our duties towards its conservation and care.

And we must add to this influence our now taken-for-granted awareness of our kinship with other animals, and the extent to which we share the DNA of even the humble fruit-fly, let alone the great apes. There is every reason, then, to demote us from the artificial throne upon which the Judaeo-Christian tradition and Descartes between them had placed us. But we must not be carried away. We may be forgiven for saying that we must keep our heads. Was Cartesian dualism truly a 'murderous dissection' of man from nature, as I have quoted Jonathan Bate as saying (see chapter 6)? That we feel ourselves more deeply embedded in our environment, a material part of the planet along with other things, by no means entails that the other things in the world are like us in every respect. In ejecting the ghost from the machine, we are not throwing out the concept of mind itself, only identifying it differently. The mind is the human capacity to do a vast variety of things that other entities cannot do. Chief among these is the capacity to use language, and through language to talk, whether to ourselves (for of course we may choose to keep some of our thinking hidden) or to others; and we can talk not only about our immediate and current experience, but about the state of the world, about global warming or about human rights. It is manifestly the case that not every thing, nor any other thing in the world can do this. To say that everything has a mind in the sense of this capacity, or that everything thinks, is to speak nonsense. We can imagine pots and pans talking, but they cannot imagine their doing so.

No more does this newly accepted conviction that man is part and parcel of the rest of nature go any way to underpinning the belief that nature as a whole is one organism with one life, the goddess Gaia. The Gaia hypothesis, while posing as science, is in fact an attempt to reintroduce the so-called spiritual element into man's relation with nature while removing the domination that the Jewish and Christian God bestowed on him. There is nothing in the new revolt against dualism to justify this move. Spiritual or 'deep' ecology is not vindicated, still less entailed by the removal of Cartesian dualism from our framework of thought. Nor, even if it were, is it obvious that, except in the case of fervent believers, it would serve as a motive for a radical change in behaviour. We are told that the Gaia theory brings back the sacred into our dealings with nature. But when it comes to practicality, though the people who work or climb mountains in Antarctica may regard it as almost sacred territory, its environmental purity regarded with awe and to be preserved from pollution at all costs, elsewhere in the world development is still regarded as a goal to be aimed for, even with the pollution that inevitably attends it.

The idea of 'sustainable development', the mantra of politicians, development, that is, which leaves an area with no worse pollution than before development began, seems a contradiction in terms. For example, the World Trade Organization, a group of 153 countries (that is three-quarters of the countries in the world), in its mission statement of 2012, surpassed itself in giving with one hand and taking back with the other:

> [All countries should] work towards raising standards of living, ensuring full employment and a large and steadily growing volume of real income and effective demand, and expanding the production of and trade in goods and services . . . with the objective of sustainable development, seeking both to protect and preserve the environment, and to enhance the means for doing so in a manner consistent with their different needs and concerns at different levels of economic development.[23]

Quite so. Development and environmental preservation are both admirable goals, no doubt, and should be pursued by countries in accordance with their levels of development; but suppose they are incompatible? The statement is like an endless boring ping-pong rally, which will go on until one party is exhausted. However this may be, the demands of economic short-term advantage, greed and the human reluctance to give up technological advances once discovered, or comforts and luxuries once enjoyed, seem likely always to outweigh at least the demands of the goddess Gaia, whatever less fanciful considerations may be pitted against them.

Yet, though all that is true, it is hard to deny that our changed view of what it is to be human, whether this has been derived from philosophy or from the biological sciences, has brought about genuine changes in our attitude to environmental values as a whole.

---

[23] Quoted in 'CAP Reform 2014–2020. Agreement and Implementation in the UK and Ireland', a paper published by the House of Commons Library, November 2013.

Even the European Common Agricultural Policy, which used to pay subsidies to farmers based on output, and which led to vast overproduction, pollution by fertilisers and the destruction of wildlife habitats (especially hedgerows and copses), has changed and is changing in directions intended to be more environmentally friendly, favouring less the American-style factory farm, and distributing subsidies better among small farmers. In the latest reform agreement for the 2014–20 period, individual countries are to have more flexibility in implementing the reforms; and so-called 'greening', the enhancement of the environment of farming, is an important element in the reforms themselves. Greening consists of the diversification of crops, the retention of permanent grassland and the special protection of ecological focus areas. The National Farmers' Union have expressed fears that the UK will use the new flexibility to prioritise greening and that profitability will come a poor second.[24] Environmentalists will have to try to keep these factors in balance.

We have come a long way in the last fifty or sixty years. We do not yet exercise the responsibilities that would go with ownership of the planet, but because we now know ourselves to inhabit it in a new way, and we realise more sharply how we affect it by our interventions, we feel far more responsibility than we used to. In the next chapter of my inquiry, I shall tentatively look ahead, and try to do so without having recourse to the metaphor of stewardship or the invention of new gods.

---

[24] Ibid., p. 17.

8. What can be done? Some useful compromises

It will, I hope, have become clear in the preceding chapters that I take a generally favourable view of ownership. I believe that it can carry with it a love of the thing owned that can be both richly enjoyable to the owner and more widely beneficent. A thing that is loved and cared for is not only protected from harm, but may be more positively developed or improved, for a more general good.

However, no one can deny that private ownership is a political matter that divides the right from the left. The gap that separates rich from poor, the haves from the have-nots, is growing wider, both within individual countries (most certainly in the UK), and across the world, dividing rich countries from poor. To take one small example, in Scotland more than half the land is owned by fewer than five hundred people, the largest landowner being the Duke of Buccleuch, who owns 240,000 acres, worth nearly £1 billion. The ancient aristocratic families who own such vast estates tend to argue in their own defence that much of the land is unproductive wilderness, and that only they understand how to look after it, and the game-birds whose habitat it is, and whose shooting brings huge revenue to the country (this last point, however, is of less significance than it would be if the owners were not, many of them, so adept at tax evasion). However, the Scottish parliament in 2010 set up a group to examine the situation, called the Scottish Land Reform Review Group, which is advocating the absolute right of tenant farmers to buy their farms, whatever the wishes of the landlords, and this would of course involve primary legislation.

Moreover, there is a growing demand for community purchase and management of parcels of land, such as has already been effected in the north west of Scotland, in Assynt and in the small island of Eigg. The ownership of Eigg was transferred to the Eigg Heritage Trust, together with the Scottish Wildlife Trust which runs it as a nature reserve, in 1997. Since then the population has risen by 24 per cent.

The trust is in receipt of lottery funds, and there have been great improvements to the harbour and to the electricity supply. It is remarkable that, in the case of the latter, most of the supply comes from wind turbines, and because it is not always adequate, a 'traffic light' system is in place, so that when the light shows red, the inhabitants restrict their use of power to the minimum. Here is an example of genuine responsibility derived from common ownership.

It seems to me that the present virtually feudal system of ownership in the rest of Scotland, which is unique in Europe, or indeed anywhere in the world, can hardly survive for ever, though not even the Scottish National Party seems to be in any hurry to legislate. Nevertheless this is an issue on which reasonable compromise must be sought. Most tenant farmers are old; few of their children or grandchildren have the inclination or the incentive to take over the farms under the current terms. Farming will become unsustainable without radical change. Such compromise, though difficult to bring about, is of course more imaginable on a domestic than a global scale. Yet perhaps some lessons may be learned from this example about what is needed to sustain a productive and benign environment, by changing the rights of those who inhabit it.

For, in the UK as a whole, the only changes in rights to be brought about in recent years are those contained in the Countryside Act 2000, the so-called 'right to roam' legislation (see chapter 1, above). But though the legislation was greeted with horror by many (including me) because it seemed to overturn rights inherent in ownership, in fact it turned out to be little more than an attempt to reinstate many ancient rights of way, and to prohibit owners from closing them off, except in certain specific circumstances, such as the game-breeding seasons. And even this legislation has now been modified so as to permit owners to divert rights of way if they pass through gardens or farmyards. So things have probably not turned out too badly. All the same, the Act was not designed to cure the evils of the paucity of ownership, nor to address the increasing plight of tenant farms, not only in Scotland, though especially there. Instead of a general and ill-thought-out entitlement of anybody to walk over and risk damaging land which they do not own, and for whose care they have no share in the responsibility, there should be a coherent and far more radical system of redistribution of ownership (nothing to do with rights of way) which would entitle individual tenant farmers, or rural communities, to purchase property, in specified circumstances.

This would be a compromise that would be fair and beneficial both immediately and for the future.

A different and historical example of compromise with regard to ownership within the UK is to be found in the foundation of the National Trust, in the nineteenth century. The Trust was established in 1895, by the social reformer, Octavia Hill, with Canon Hardwicke Rawnsley and her legal and financial adviser, Sir Robert Hunter, who acted as secretary to the Trust until his death. Octavia Hill had long been devoted to providing accessible open spaces inside London for the people whose housing she managed, and to whose welfare she was deeply committed. She believed in 'the life-enhancing virtues of pure earth, clean air and blue sky'. She held that the greatest need of the poor was for space, where they could enjoy fresh air, beautiful surroundings, a place where they could sit, and where their children could play. She thought of access to such an environment as a necessity for everyone, but especially for poor city-dwellers, who lived and worked in a deeply polluted atmosphere.

Octavia Hill's interest, then, was primarily in people, who, she held, should have access to an environment from which they could draw benefits both physical and psychological. Her co-founder, Canon Rawnsley, was inspired by rather different motives. He held successive ecclesiastical livings in the Lake District, to which he was passionately devoted, and where he was a Rural Dean, and Canon of Carlisle Cathedral. He was also a poet and an energetic pamphleteer and campaigner for the environmental protection of the Lake District. His campaigns were especially directed against the construction of roads and railways, which would change its character, and destroy its relatively inaccessible and remote sublimity. He was supported in these campaigns by John Ruskin, who actually suggested the title 'The National Trust' for the new organisation. The aim of the Trust was 'to buy and preserve for the benefit of the public historic places or places of natural beauty'. In 1907, on the advice of Sir Robert Hunter, a bill was introduced in parliament which would prohibit the winding up of the Trust; and The National Trust Act, which gave the Trust permanent status, became law. But the Trust remains an organisation for private ownership, outside state control.

It will be seen that from the start the Trust had a dual function, to preserve and care for historic houses, and to conserve the environment, while giving everyone access to both. The first of these had become a matter of urgency, since a philanthropist had wished to leave her house and its contents to the nation in the late 1880s, but could not do so with the safeguards that she sought, because there was no body in existence through which she could do it. On the other hand, it was to the conservation of unpolluted and undeveloped nature that Canon Rawnsley was especially committed. It was perhaps Ruskin who persuaded the original trustees to put the buildings first among their aims. At any rate this dual mission meant that the National Trust has never been primarily concerned with wilderness, or with those aspects of nature in which human beings have scarcely intervened. Many of the houses that the Trust has acquired over the years are set in beautiful (and beautifully maintained) parks or gardens. But there is no pretence that they are not the imaginative creations of man. People pay to visit these places as much for the houses and their interiors as for the outdoors; and even outside, they are as much interested in the layout of the gardens and parks, or the trees and flowers that grow there as in unspoiled nature. Moreover, the 'amenity' factor is considerable: the National Trust shops are such that the word 'dainty' might have been invented for them and the goods they sell; their cafeterias are much used and often excellent.

All the same, one must not forget what a vast amount of the coastline of England, Wales and Northern Ireland is owned by the National Trust (Scotland has its own Trust). One can, for instance, still be quite alone, buffeted by wind, one's ears assaulted by the crashing waves below, even alarmingly lost, on the sinisterly named Morte Point in North Devon. And there are hundreds of miles of such coastal walks, occasionally signposted, but otherwise maintained with the lightest touch, that are the property and responsibility of the Trust.

The National Trust now has a membership of two million. And similar trusts, modelled on it, are in existence all over the world, from the Isle of Man to the Caribbean Islands. This, then, is a compromise, a private trust that owns, conserves and cares for much of our domestic environment for the benefit of the public and of the environment itself. The Trust relies to a considerable extent on the work of volunteers, both in its gardens and in the wilder parts of the country. There is no doubt that for many people to mix their labour with something brings them a sense of ownership that is deeply satisfying, partly because of the widespread and general benefit of their work.

Besides land and buildings owned by the National Trust, there exist in England, Wales and Northern Ireland designated 'Areas of Outstanding Natural Beauty'. (In Scotland they are separately designated, and known as National Scenic Areas, overseen by the Scottish Natural Heritage.) They were first created by the National Parks and Access to the Countryside Act (1949). The Countryside and Rights of Way Act (2000) added further measures to protect them as a national resource. They make up 18 per cent of the country, and they are managed by local authorities, or other local and community bodies such as the conservation boards which may be set up under the provisions of the 2000 Act and which must be formed mostly from local people. A National Association of Areas of Outstanding Natural Beauty was established in 1998 as an independent body to look after the interests of the areas in England and Wales; this body was among the casualties of the cull of independent bodies carried out in 2011, and its functions have now been transferred to Whitehall. It is too early to tell whether this has done any harm. Although the word 'beauty' is part of the name of these areas, the criteria for designation are not solely aesthetic. They include the quality of the flora and fauna and even of the human communities to be found within it (though I am not quite sure by what standards these last are judged: I suppose a long history of human settlement might be one criterion, and the absence of factory farming another). There is, of course, much overlap between the Areas of Outstanding Natural Beauty and the land and properties owned by the National Trust, many of which fall within such areas. Much of the coastline, for example, is protected both as Trust property and as an Area of Natural Beauty.

Another form of compromise conservation is, or perhaps should be, the 13 per cent of land that has been designated 'Green-Belt' land outside cities, protected against ribbon development alongside roadways. However, by 2013 the government had announced highly controversial plans to allow housing development in green-belt areas, subject to local planning permissions. It would seem to me far more rational to meet the, admittedly acute, housing shortage by intense urban development, which in the twenty-first century could be built to far higher standards than were the disastrous post-Second World War tower blocks. But it is probably true that the English are reluctant apartment-dwellers; Octavia Hill did her work too well, in making them desire access not only to city parks, but to their own gardens and to the countryside. Nevertheless, green-belt development will almost certainly have a harmful effect on the environment, since it will inevitably entail greater levels of emission of CO_2 gas into the atmosphere, through the greater use of cars (to say nothing of petrol-driven lawn-mowers), while more intense urban development would have the opposite effect. It is remarkable how many (especially childless) urban dwellers do not run a car. How much damage will be done will largely depend on the political colour of the different local authorities involved, as well as on the development of electric-powered cars. But, whatever happens next, in its original intention the creation of the Green Belt was another measure of compromise conservation, restricting by law to what use the protected land might be put.

In 2012 Roger Scruton, the philosopher and aesthetician, published a book entitled *Green Philosophy: How to Think Seriously about the Planet*,[1] a passionate defence of individual and local community involvement with the local environment (including, but not restricted to, the private ownership of property), as the only way to combat environmental destruction on a global scale. His enemies are state ownership, and those Green environmental theories which advocate worldwide interventions dictated by some central authority, and agreed at climate summits. Such measures, Scruton argues, in the unlikely event of their ever being agreed, would lead to the kind of bureaucracy in which nobody takes final responsibility, and corruption is rife. Scruton is full of praise for the National Trust and other organisations set up to conserve the countryside and its wildlife habitats, or to encourage people to enjoy it. He holds that such organisations exemplify a virtue which he names 'oikophilia', the love of home; for 'home' may mean either literally one's own dwelling place, or one's neighbourhood, or the country that is one's own. The National Trust makes people feel that the history of the English country is theirs, and the English countryside itself, and causes them to value it as such. The same is true of the many other national trusts, each one of which is established in a place that is 'oikos' to different people. Such love of home mirrors the love and pride that people may

---

[1] Roger Scruton, *Green Philosophy: How to Think Seriously about the Planet* (Atlantic Books, London 2012).

feel where their own property is concerned. It is only from oikophilia, so Scruton argues, that will arise the sense of responsibility which alone will protect a particular environment from harm. But oikophilia is necessarily geographically limited.

It will come as no surprise that I accept the strong connection that Scruton makes between ownership and responsibility. But I part company from him in so far as he denies the possibility, or indeed the desirability, of extending such responsibility beyond the 'oikos'. It is not that he denies the existence of climate change and its disastrous consequences for the planet as a whole. He is no Nigel Lawson, the former Chancellor of the Exchequer, now a Conservative peer, and the devoter of great energy to climate change denying. It is simply that he does not believe in the feasibility of securing cooperation between all the different nations involved, or in the efficacy of bureaucratic intervention, dictated from above, and enforced only by the feeble arm of international law. Such attempts at transnational legislation or treaty are, he believes, doomed to failure, and to the deterioration of conditions overall. And it is true that all such summits have ended in failure.

Scruton's argument is partly based on an analogy with the EU. One persuasive example is of EU regulations regarding the packaging of food. It is worth quoting at length:

> All over Europe fields, rivers, lakes and hedgerows are filling with plastic bottles and bags, and the per capita production of plastic waste ranges from 100 kilograms in Finland to more than double that amount in France. Yet what is the reaction of the EU? To require all food to be packaged before it can leave the farm; to lay down stringent health and safety regulations that cannot be met by small local shops, so that food must be centrally processed and packaged in plastic; to oblige manufacturers to wrap detailed instructions in ten languages along with all their products; and in general to force upon producers and consumers a culture of litter and waste. No national government that wished now to get rid of non-biodegradable packaging, to return to the benign regime of sweets in paper bags, fish in newspaper or pickled beets in barrels could adopt such a policy. All governments throughout the union have been locked into policies concerning the production and distribution of food which, though they may enhance the health of present consumers, have a long-term environmental cost that will far outweigh the short-term benefits.[2]

---

[2] Ibid., pp. 115–16.

As one who struggles daily with plastic packaging, and who lives in a part of London where every stream, gutter and hedgerow is contaminated with discarded plastic bottles and bags, I have great sympathy with this outburst. Yet, though I do not deny, and have repeatedly asserted, the obstacles in the way of extending the idea of responsibility beyond the area where ownership requires it, I do not believe that the analogy of EU bureaucracy should deter us from seeking international solutions to what is an international problem. I shall return to this crucial subject below.

Meanwhile, in any case, I find that there is something suspect about the concept of oikophilia itself which makes it impossible for me at least to accept it as the key to a solution. My uneasiness stems, I think, from an ambiguity in the idea of 'belonging' which seems to be part of the meaning of the neologism. The oikos or home belongs to me: I own it. Even if in law I only possess it, I have made it my own, and therefore, as I have argued, I love it and feel responsible for it, and I am potentially proud of it, in a special way. But, on the other hand, I belong to it; it is where I am at home. This is a different and a powerful concept, and one which is enormously important for human wellbeing, especially in the case of children. Many emotionally fragile children, for example, cannot flourish in the environment of a large, impersonal school; they desperately need a small school within whose walls they feel safe, recognised, unthreatened. Children in care need a home, in this sense. They need to be adopted or fostered so that they have somewhere where they belong. I certainly do not deny the value that we attach to feeling at home, to belonging in this way, nor do I deny that many of us feel that we most belong when we are settled in a place on earth that belongs to us, whose ownership we claim. Scruton, however, appears to derive our sense of responsibility essentially from the value of belonging rather than that of owning. And here I think that perhaps he has learned too much from the phenomenology of Martin Heidegger. Although he is rightly critical of the obfuscating jargon in which Heidegger wraps his thought, he nevertheless accepts in full the value designated in German as *Heimatlichkeit*, the feeling for settled home territory, which for Heidegger defines the proper relation between human beings and their environment.

Scruton argues that environmentalists have unduly neglected this value, and in this he is perhaps right. But this may be explained, in part at least, by the strong association of *Heimatlichkeit* with the idea of the 'homeland', a concept that had been a staple component of Nazi propaganda and indeed practice from 1933 onwards (and Heidegger had been a Nazi). *Heimatlichkeit* implies continuity in time as well as 'settledness' in space; and Green politicians and environmentalist philosophers in Germany, where their influence was early and strong after the Second World War, though they could articulate Green policies in terms of the future, could not easily confront the history of Germany or the historical sense of 'belonging' and 'not belonging', so recently and appallingly exemplified in the Holocaust. Even now, eighty years after Hitler's coming to power, there still remains an aftertaste of antisemitism, a whiff of disagreeable xenophobia about *Heimatlichkeit* and thus about 'oikophilia'. You don't want strangers or people who don't 'belong' trampling all over your lovely home.

Let us abandon oikophilia, then, and with it, as far as we can, the left/right polarisation of private ownership. Let us accept that private ownership of things is on the whole beneficent, and in any case is extraordinarily difficult to eliminate. It lies at the heart of civilised society and is enshrined in the law. It is with us to stay, as are its associated virtues and vices. Its associated virtues are generosity and good husbandry. Its associated vices are miserliness and, far and away more damaging and commoner, greed. It is time now to return to the unanswered question: how are we to take responsibility for exercising the virtues associated with ownership and curbing the vices, at an international level?

For there can be no doubt that it needs to be done. We probably all have our own especial nightmare when our minds turn to pollution. Mine is concerned with the tonnes of electronic waste regularly exported from the UK to Africa and elsewhere in the developing world. Electronic devices become more and more sophisticated, and when something new comes on the market, its predecessor is discarded. One's computer is constantly being updated, whether one wants it or not, and the hardware does not keep up with the software. The average life of a new computer, smart phone, tablet or digital camera, is two years. They are deliberately designed so that they will not last, and cannot be either repaired or recycled. When the discarded monsters (though mostly very small and sleek, they are monstrous in the damage they do) arrive at their destination in the poor countries to which they are shipped, they are picked over carefully for anything that may still be used, and then become landfill.

Under the ground they release their toxic content which gradually over the years seeps through the earth spreading poison as it goes, and up into the atmosphere above, slowly poisoning the inhabitants of the country in question and destroying the conditions necessary for sustaining any life. The alternative is to dump them far out to sea; but the environmental consequences are no better.

This is a typical nightmare, in which a process once started grows out of control and cannot be stopped, like the carrying of the buckets of water by the animated broomstick, in the Sorcerer's Apprentice, or like Frankenstein's Monster. As a child I was prey to such nightmares, taking hours to get over them (as was one of my children), and they were made worse by the presence on their dream scene of a circle of people sitting doing their knitting, not noticing that something terrible was going on.

But in this case, we can break out of the nightmare, and must do so as a matter of urgency: legislation must be introduced to compel manufacturers to spend a proportion of their profits on research and development whose sole aim will be to produce electronic objects capable of being recycled. They would not be permitted to market a new product unless they could demonstrate that they were genuinely carrying out such research. If this slowed down the production of new gadgets, all to the good. But the market would provide an incentive to comply.

This would be a measure that an individual government in an individual country could take, yet with the aim of remedying a situation in countries other than its own. It would accord with the principle enshrined in the Environmental Protection Act 1990 that the polluter pays; and it would extend responsibility for the avoidance of harm beyond the 'oikos' to which Roger Scruton seems to wish to confine it. Not everything that we own is nice or a cause of pride. Some of it is nasty and should make us ashamed. We own the waste that we create, and must take responsibility for it, as well as for our flower gardens.

I advocate such domestic yet outward-looking legislation since, reluctantly, I have come to share Scruton's scepticism about the efficacy of global summits, in Copenhagen, Warsaw or anywhere else. What is the point of the United Nations expensively seeking agreement round the table, when it has been shown time and again that no country is prepared to sacrifice its own current economic recovery or future growth for the sake of the planet? I used to be inclined to argue that, the United Nations, with all its ineptitude, being the only thing we had, we should continue to try to bring about agreements, treaties and even international laws, for the good of the world. In the different context of peacekeeping, I suppose I would still deploy my old somewhat lack-lustre argument, though with ever-decreasing conviction; but in the context of global warming and the future of the planet, I seem to have lost that shred of hope.

Are we cast back, then, on the apparently extremely modest remedies, suggested almost forty years ago by John Passmore (see chapter 7, above), namely research and education? I believe that we are. In an article in *The Times* of 18 November 2013, Professor Bjorn Lomborg, Director of the Copenhagen Consensus Centre, a think-tank of economists advising governments on how best to spend money to save the world, wrote 'The last twenty years of international climate negotiations have achieved almost nothing, and have done so at enormous economic cost'. She goes on to congratulate Japan for abandoning the target of 25 per cent reduction in greenhouse gas emissions below the 1990 level by 2020. They have declared that this is unattainable, and that emissions will actually rise by 3 per cent in this time. They have, however, undertaken to spend $110 billion over the next five years, from a mix of public and private sources, on innovation in environmental and energy technologies. This will provide the motivation for Japan to benefit itself and the rest of the world as well. It is domestic policy directed outwards. And this, as I have already suggested, seems to be the only way forward.

Yet the policy of climate summits remains exactly as it was at the failed summit of Kyoto and that of Copenhagen, its rhetoric and arbitrary targets unchanged, nations promising reductions and then pulling out or simply failing to meet the target. And the attempts at reduction by the use of renewable sources of energy have been enormously expensive and inefficient, because the technology has not been properly developed and tested before being put into use.

Poor countries cannot possibly be expected to sign up to policies which are bound to increase not only the cost of domestic fuel, but also the cost of manufacturing and food production and thus the size of all household bills. When Passmore wrote of the need for more research, the urgency of that need was not so clear, nor the disastrous consequences of neglecting it. It is time that other countries, including the UK, followed the example that Japan has set, not overlooking the outrage that is expressed by Green protesters against Japan's retreat from its target, but rationally arguing in terms of cost/benefit.

And there is already hope that research can produce results. While the UK has lagged behind other European countries in turning carbon-containing waste (including kitchen and farm waste and sewage) by a process known as anaerobiotic digestion (AD) into a low-grade kind of fuel (the UK uses 49 per cent of such waste as landfill; Germany and the Netherlands use none), a new biochemical process has been developed which can turn such waste into high-grade fuel such as can be used in jet-aircraft. I quote from Lord Krebs, speaking in the House of Lords in December 2014, to introduce the report of the Select Committee on Science and Technology, entitled 'Waste or Resource?' (Hansard Grand Committee, column 491):

> By harnessing the power of biological chemistry it is possible to reassemble waste into valuable products. . . . This is not just a gleam in the scientists' eye. The technology for some of these transformations already exists, and for others it is within reach in the next few years. We [The Committee] heard of one industrial-scale example already in practice, a partnership between Virgin Atlantic and LanzaTech to use bacteria to convert carbon monoxide waste gas from steel mills into jet fuel. LanzaTech estimates that 19% of the world's jet fuel demands could be met by this technology, which has a carbon footprint of probably around half that of conventional jet fuel.

If the UK would back this new technology, even though it would be initially costly, the effects on carbon emissions worldwide would be profound.

Moreover, apart from the need for the kinds of research that I have mentioned, more research is needed into affordable energy-saving house-building. Although one frequently reads accounts of new buildings that are miracles of warmth and comfort without pollution, and though we are bombarded with advice about how to improve the energy efficiency of our own homes, the standards are still low, the innovative construction techniques still rare. Spending on research and development in the construction industry should become mandatory.

When we turn to Passmore's other remedy, education, I think we can see again that things have changed. The time that he wrote his book was well into the period when primary school children were being taught that morality was a matter of other people carrying out deplorable practices such as factory farming or the destruction of rainforests. Teachers who had been educated in the 1950s and 1960s were afraid of mentioning right and wrong behaviour that was nearer to the classroom and playground, lest they might seem 'judgemental', or to be seeking to 'indoctrinate' children, who should be allowed to form their own views of good and evil. And they were taught to be especially wary, in what was becoming an increasingly multicultural society. It was far safer to discuss matters of which children would have no direct experience, and where questions of personal responsibility, or of resisting the temptation to do wrong, did not arise. (And without the idea of resisting temptation, it seems to me, there can be no moral sense.) The children had not cut down a rainforest, nor ever been tempted to do so. At this time the harms being done to the environment were, as we have seen, beginning to be widely acknowledged, and seemed to be exempt from the kind of moral relativism that was still rampant among teachers. They could be roundly condemned, with impunity. At this stage, before the introduction of a subject called Citizenship, a bit more oikophilia would have come in useful: children were seldom taught to be vigilant about litter (though it must be said that schools differed very widely on this issue), or to be loving of their own immediate environment.

Now, however, even primary school children are taught far more of the science of global warming and climate change. They know far more about ecological interdependence, food chains and the effects of chemical pollution. Indeed, I doubt whether anything has changed in education more than the teaching of science in primary schools, and very properly this teaching begins and often ends with the teaching of the environmental and biological sciences. This has meant that, as a young person's education proceeds, the essentially political issue of policy concerning the global environment can be discussed against a background of some understanding of the facts. Or so one would hope. But, as is the rule with political matters, prejudgement and party loyalty tend to outweigh evidence, and I believe that much more can be done to educate opinion, teach people to weigh up evidence, and provide them with opportunities to gain experience of different environmental conditions, both inside and outside school.

For example, loosely based on and replacing the post-Second

World War idea of 'twinning' towns and villages with counterparts in Europe with whom they were expected to develop a special connection, there has grown up since 2002 an organisation called BUILD. This stands for Building Understanding through International Links for Development, and the links are between the UK and the 'global South', that is Africa, India, the Caribbean and South America. The links are known as partnerships, and are mainly between individual schools, colleges, hospitals, professional organisations and faith groups. The partnerships receive modest government subsidy, though their funding is largely dependent on local support; and they make considerable use of volunteers. Their aim is to increase mutual understanding, and development in such fields as the training of teachers and of physicians and surgeons, and in public health. Both members of the partnerships spend time working in each other's country. This is important in so far as it distances BUILD from the lopsided relationship of foreign aid, about which both taxpayers at home and those who hope to receive aid abroad are becoming increasingly disenchanted. It introduces an element of mutuality, which, as we have seen, brings with it a sense of responsibility. At the AGM of the All-Party Parliamentary Group on Connecting Communities in 2008, Archbishop Desmond Tutu said 'You are saying "we are family". If we don't listen and respond to that call, we are destined for extinction'. I believe that there is scope for considerably extending this kind of partnership, which is, in a highly practical way, educational, leading as it does not only to mutual understanding but also to shared activity.

It is as true of education as it is of research that one cannot predict its outcome. But, in my opinion, research and education together will probably lead us slowly in the direction of the goal: that we assume common responsibility for the world that we do not own, which lies beyond our backyard but which we jointly inhabit; and I also believe that nothing else will do so.

9. Why do we want to preserve the natural world?

I now come to the final, and more properly philosophical question in my reflections on ownership. It is easy to see why we want to conserve or protect that which we own; but why do we want to do the same for anything that is not ours, including the planet on which, through no choice of our own, we happen to live? Of course we may hope that it will last our time. But why would it seem wrong to say 'Après moi, le déluge', and give the matter no further thought? Is it out of sympathy with those comparatively few people who we know will survive us, such as younger friends and members of our own close family? But then everyone's motive would be different, their interest in the matter differently limited; and some would have no motive at all. Is it, then, out of a sense of moral obligation? And if so, to whom? I have, I think, implicitly given, or at least suggested, my answer to this question in the course of my arguments above; but it deserves a somewhat more thorough account before the investigation is closed.

First, it will doubtless have been observed that in considering things that I do not own, I have sometimes been concerned with landscape and habitat, both wild and cultivated, which, as it were domestically, we wish to preserve through such organisations as the National Trust. We wish to preserve these places because we value them and love them, not only in our own country, though (and I concede this much to Roger Scruton) perhaps especially there. We value such spaces, unowned by us, not only if we are familiar with them (though, again, especially when we are) but where we have no direct acquaintance with them. When, in 2011, the government published a plan to sell off 250,000 hectares of state-owned woodland, including the Forest of Dean, more than half a million people signed a petition opposing the sale, and the plan was abandoned. A similar plan was announced, at the beginning of 2014, to permit the destruction of some ancient forests for building development, but this time with the proviso that the developers are mandated to plant 100 trees within the vicinity, for every tree felled. It is too early to predict the fate of this plan, but it will doubtless be opposed by many conservationists. The planting of new woods, however desirable, cannot replace ancient woodland whose soil surrounding old trees has been relatively undisturbed for years, and has developed unique nutritional and ecological characteristics, like giant compost heaps. This kind of ancient woodland, wooded for 400 years or more, is habitat for numbers of endangered species of animals, insects and plants and is widely valued beyond price. But, like all woodland, it needs to be managed. Much of it has lost its environmental value through neglect. There are numerous laws and regulations covering both the UK and the EU that are designed to protect particular species of trees, many of which are found in ancient woodland, but perhaps governments should give more attention to grading ancient woodland, and protecting especially the richest in species diversity.[1] For, after all, well-managed woods, of whatever age, along with open grassland and coastal paths, are all of them rightly valued highly. They are what most people think of as making up 'the country', much of which is, on the whole happily, preserved by the compromises of the National Trust, the scheme of Areas of Outstanding Natural Beauty, and by specially dedicated bodies such as the Woodland Trust, the Royal Society for the Protection of Birds, as well as by private property owners. If we join some of these organisations, or name them in our wills, we are taking shared responsibility for that which we value, in so far as their conservation is paid for with our money; and if we volunteer to work for, say, the National Trust, it may be a relatively active share. Such has formed one part of what I have been concerned with, in considering problems of preserving what we do not own.

In other contexts, however, I have been concerned with the world as a whole, that is, with no less than the preservation of the planet. What is perceived as at risk, here, is not just the habitats of some endangered species of animals and plants, or countryside that is pleasing to the eye (though these things are also at risk), but the very conditions that sustain life of any kind whatever. With the exception

---

[1] For a recent useful, though inconclusive discussion of ancient woodland, see POSTnote no. 465 Parliamentary Office of Science and Technology, June 2014.

of Roger Scruton, who begs us to concentrate on what lies near home, most philosophers who have considered the ethics of environmental preservation have switched back and forth between these two aspects of the matter. What the two different objects of concern have in common is, obviously, their vulnerability to being spoiled, whether by deliberate change of use, or by the careless disposal of waste, or by largely manmade emissions bringing about climate change, and all its consequences.

I think it is defensible to raise the question of our motivation to save the environment under these two aspects without making a sharp or absolute distinction between them, because whichever aspect we consider, and however wide or narrow our concern, our environment is subject to similar risks; but I shall argue that, in the end, our motivation for engaging in their protection is different.

However, I must first get out of the way a suggested motivation that would, if it were intelligible, apply to both aspects equally. As I have already said, I do not believe we are motivated to conservationism by a sense of duty to those who will succeed us as inhabitants of the planet. This is partly because one cannot have a duty or obligation to an indefinite or infinite class of people. It is commonly held that you ought to do something only if it is in your power to do it ('ought implies can', as moral philosophers are inclined to say), and it is not within your power to do something for the indefinite number of people who may, or may not, exist in the future.

Perhaps I should say that I do not, as a matter of fact, put much weight on the saying 'ought implies can'. This is not because I believe one can have infinite duties, but because of the inherent ambiguity of 'ought'. If I have promised to meet your train, but, in going out to my car, I slip and break my pelvis, there is a sense in which, because I have promised, I ought to be on my way to the station. Instead I am lying on the ice; I cannot get up. And doubtless my knowledge that you will be expecting me is part of my misery. In another sense, that I ought to be there to meet you is cancelled by my inability to do so, and you will understand this when you learn the facts, and not blame me. Understood in this way, it is nonsense to say that I ought to have done what I could not do. What I ought to do is not necessarily the same as what I can rightly be blamed for failing to do.

It is not, however, only on the grounds that I cannot have an indefinite duty that I reject the motivation of obligation to future generations. It is rather that, while the idea of conserving things for future people is familiar enough, it does not seem to apply to this case. I may write into my will that a certain one of my pictures shall go to my eldest son. But the trouble with this familiar idea is that it seems to have application only in the case of ownership, of disposing of things that I own, or of holding them in trust: and what we are considering here is, specifically, things that we do not own, nor, except metaphorically, hold in trust.

A bold attempt to answer the question that forms the title to this chapter was made thirty years ago. In 1984 Derek Parfit published a book about the idea of personal identity.[2] In the introduction to the book he writes:

> My two subjects, reasons and persons, have close connections. I believe that most of us have false beliefs about our own nature, and our identity over time, and that when we see the truth we ought to change some of our beliefs about what we have reason to do.[3]

Most people think (and I must admit at once that I obstinately continue to think) that their identity is that of a living material body, born at a particular time and dying at a particular time. I have reasons for acting in my own interest (though not, as a matter of fact, exclusively in my own interest) and this includes the interests of me as I assume I shall be in the future, my future self as well as my immediately present self. For example, I have reason to get my roof mended now, because 'I-now' am suffering from leaks in my loft; but I also have reason to take out insurance that will cover any future leaks, from which I-now am not yet suffering but will suffer if the roof-mending has not been properly carried out. I have reason to save for my old age, and to make a will to ensure that my possessions are distributed in the way that I now want. If I am wealthy, I may found an institution in my name that will continue with charitable or research work that I have done, and which I-now wish to continue to be done. But I shall no longer be there to see it when I die. This is what we assume. I can imagine, and like to think of, a future without me, but in which the trees I carefully planted are enjoyed by my descendants, or the research done in my name goes on bearing fruit. But this imagined future is just that: imagined.

---

[2] Derek Parfit, *Reasons and Persons* (Oxford University Press, Oxford 1984).

[3] Ibid., p. ix.

Parfit, however, thinks that such common-sense beliefs are false and should be given up. Instead of the relation between myself now and my past and future selves being a relation of physical, self-renewing, continuity over a definite though unpredictable period of time, and therefore a serial, one–one relationship, me-yesterday, to me-today, to me-tomorrow, he holds that personal identity is a psychological, branching, one–many relationship and is a matter of degree. Thus in the future, there will exist thoughts, memories, preferences, psychological states that are identical with mine, and others that are identical with those of other people. Collectively, you and I and all the rest of us now alive are continuous with the future people with whom we share some of our psychological states. If we hold this view of personal identity with future selves, we shall in one way be making our thoughts, both about the present and about the future, more impersonal, that is, less confined to our own person (in the normal sense), or to a particular existing space or time. They will not even be confined to those future people whom we may think of as our genetic descendants, and who may have inherited certain psychological dispositions in the genes that came from us. Thus our reason for wishing to preserve the planet for the future becomes a kind of collective desire for self-preservation. All of us-now have reason to preserve us-then because we-now shall to some extent actually be we-then. Perhaps people who are taught by their religion to believe in reincarnation may feel a bit like this about future people.

I may have misrepresented Parfit's argument; I have certainly tried to simplify it. I cannot accept it, largely because I am so deeply committed to the ordinary way of thinking, but partly also because he invites us to abandon the common way of thinking by means of a series of thought experiments which I am incapable of carrying out. For instance (and again I am simplifying), we are to imagine a person, John, who has died, but immediately after his death his brain was removed, sliced and transplanted into the bodies of two or more other people. These other people will share some of John's memories, preferences and so on and will therefore be John, as well as still being Tom, Dick, or Harry, because, in sharing his brain, they share some of his actual brain-states, which appear in them as memories and other psychological experiences. Although Parfit is careful to explain his thought-experiments in relation to changes in consciousness experienced by actual patients following actual brain surgery, this does not allow me to adopt or even consider adopting a concept of a thus branching personal identity so remote from common sense. I am constantly brought up short by the thought that this cannot be; it is fantasy. And I cannot change my ingrained way of thinking on the basis of science fiction.

The philosopher P.F. Strawson once remarked in interview that there are two kinds of philosophy, descriptive and revisionary. Descriptive philosophy lays bare what we instinctively think, or what is embedded in our language, and explains what lies at its core (and one of his own most illuminating works was subtitled 'an essay in descriptive metaphysics'). Revisionary philosophy, on the other hand, aims to change these embedded core assumptions, as Kant asked us to stop thinking of our minds passively receiving impressions from the world and to think instead of our minds creating the world as we know it. Parfit is undoubtedly a revisionist. And though I cannot follow him, I admire his serious attempt to answer the question I am now asking, namely how are we to find motives or reasons to save the planet?

In 1992, Bernard Williams published a short essay entitled 'Must a concern for the environment be centred on human beings?'[4] I have already quoted from this essay (see chapter 6, above). In it, he directly addresses my question, and concludes that what is basic to any motive for conservation of the natural world for the future is, not so much an altruistic concern for other people yet to be born, as 'a sense of restraint in the face of nature'. And such a sense of restraint, he holds, is grounded in what he calls 'Promethean Fear',

> a fear of taking too lightly or inconsiderately our relations to nature. On this showing, the grounds of our attitudes will be very different from that suggested by any appeal to the interests of natural things [including human beings]. It will not be an extension of benevolence or altruism, nor directly will it be a sense of community . . . It will be based rather on a sense of an opposition between ourselves and nature, as an old, unbounded and potentially dangerous enemy, which requires respect. 'Respect' is the notion that perhaps more than any other needs examination here – and not . . . in the sense of respect for a sovereign, but that in which we have a healthy respect for mountainous terrain or treacherous seas.

---

[4] First published in *Ethics and the Environment*, C.C.W. Taylor (ed.) (Oxford University Press, Oxford 1992). Reprinted in Bernard Williams, *Making Sense of Humanity and Other Philosophical Papers* (Cambridge University Press, Cambridge 1995).

In 1999, David Wiggins took up the challenge to examine the idea of respect, in his Presidential Lecture to the Aristotelian Society, Respect for Nature,[5] in which he elaborated further on Williams's essay. He starts with a long quotation from an essay written by a Cambridgeshire farmer, Robin Page,[6] which is a passionate lament for the loss of wildlife, and especially birds and their habitats, from the fields and farms of Cambridgeshire – no more breeding swallows, barn owls, larks or lapwings, no more otters or harvest mice. Wiggins, following Williams, regards this lament as the articulation of a value that human beings hold strongly; they place value on the very existence of such aspects of the natural world, apart from any utility they may have for themselves and other human beings, and apart from any dangers their loss may pose for biodiversity (Wiggins dismisses with scorn the idea that biodiversity might be an intrinsic value, and I agree with him. It is the sound of the lark ascending, a sound my grandchildren have never heard, that one loves and that used to lift one's heart, not an ecological concept).

The difficulty, as both Wiggins and Williams note, is to incorporate this value in political action plans; and this is because politics is to a large extent governed by the advice of economists. Economists think of human beings as driven by preferences that can be quantified. So the cost/benefit analysis that is supposed to precede decisions of policy, for example the decision to build over ancient woodlands, can be expressed in monetary terms. How much would you pay for the retaining of the woodland? Or what would you accept as compensation for its loss? It is true that welfare economists are prepared to concede that there are some things in the world that have 'existence value', as opposed to the 'exchange value' of commodities such as food or fuel; but, in order to pursue their trade at all, they have to attempt to put a price on these things as well, to make them commensurate with those other goods that people prefer. This they tend to do by referring to the valued features as 'amenities'. A clean beach or the spectacle of puffins nesting on Sumborough Head in the Shetland Isles are 'amenities'. They may argue that if puffins are not endangered but flourish, say, in Iceland, they have no 'amenity

[5] *The Proceedings of the Aristotelian Society* (London 2000).

[6] Robin Page, 'Restoring the countryside in town and country', in A. Barnett and R. Scruton (eds), *Town and Country* (Jonathan Cape, London 1998).

value', and need not be expensively preserved. But the economists are wrong: nothing would compensate me for the loss of the puffins at Sumborough Head; nothing could be weighed in the balance against the Cambridgeshire farmer's loss of the larks, swallows and lapwings. It is an absolute loss, and the way in which the significance of his life is diminished is irreparable, unless nature can be restored. Roger Scruton sums it up: 'Moral reasoning is not economic reasoning. In moral reasoning we are not trading preferences, but safeguarding the things that cannot be traded'.[7]

Although I observed above that policy-makers tend to be led by the cost/benefit analysis of economists, it is worth noticing the increasing number of laws and regulations that parliament passes which reflect values that apparently override economic calculations, or treat them as irrelevant. This may be termed 'moral legislation' and is typically concerned with human life or death. For example, the policy which, in certain circumstances, permits life-support to be withdrawn from a child, or further surgery withheld, is based on arguments concerned with the avoidance of further suffering, or on the quality of life the patient might expect, not on the manifestly cogent consideration of cost to the NHS of keeping the child alive. Again, it is widely taken for granted that monetary considerations should never trump arguments derived from human dignity and compassion, in the provision of care for the aged. As dangers to the environment become better understood and more urgent, perhaps 'green' values may begin to have similar weight, as seems to have been the case in the withdrawal of the plan to sell the Forest of Dean for development.

To return to Wiggins's lecture, because it was structured round Mr Page's lament, he introduces late in his argument, and as a second aspect of 'respect' for nature, an aspect mentioned only in a few lines by Page, but central to Bernard Williams's concept of respect. This is that feeling which should restrain us from making rash assaults on nature, or making light of its powers; the respect we pay to a strong and largely unpredictable enemy.

Wiggins's example of failure in such 'respect' is the outrage committed in 1987 by the manufacturers of cattle feed. Cattle feed is

---

[7] Roger Scruton, *Green Philosophy: How to Think Seriously about the Planet* (Atlantic Books, London 2012) p. 201.

generally given bulk by the addition of soya bean flour; but soya beans do not grow well in Europe, and must be imported. So to save money and increase profits, manufacturers began to introduce sheep offal into cattle feed instead, thus turning herbivorous animals into carnivores. It was eventually discovered that it was this that led to the outbreak of BSE, or Mad Cow Disease, in that year. To bring the disease under control, thousands of cattle had to be culled. Because the incubation period is so long, cattle may be infected but show no symptoms for years, so diagnosis was at first extremely difficult. The official ban on the export of British beef was not lifted until 2006; and the sale in the UK of potentially contaminated offal such as sweetbreads and liver was prohibited and only gradually relaxed. It is still not certain (again, because of the very long incubation period) that the last human being to be infected with the related, and always fatal, Variant Creutzfeldt-Jakob Disease (vCJD) has died, though the number of cases has dropped, and the most recent deaths have been of people in their twenties, which suggests that there may be few if any older people carrying the infection undetected.

Of this outrage, Wiggins commented in his Presidential Lecture: 'the thing we need to dare to say is that this act that was done should never even have been contemplated. There was something in it that was not only mindlessly rapacious . . . but nefarious and sacrilegious'. The use of the word 'sacrilegious' is striking; Wiggins is not at all impressed by the claims of 'spiritual ecology' or the invention of new gods. But he connects the attitude towards nature that he advocates with the Roman concept of *religio* which permeates, to take one supreme example, Virgil's Georgics. It can be characterised as a mixture of restraint, that is, a limited demand for luxury and indulgence, and a peaceful and grateful enjoyment of the natural world, both cultivated and uncultivated. It is for such an attitude that he takes over Bernard Williams's word 'respect'.

I have to admit to a great dislike of the word 'respect', which is doubtless irrational, because the word can be used harmlessly enough, and the sense in which Williams and Wiggins wish to use it is perfectly harmless. But I loathe being told that I must 'respect' other people's religious faith, when that faith leads them to acts of barbaric and unlawful cruelty or appalling violence. I don't care for people who start a sentence with the words 'with respect' and then proceed to rubbish everything that I have just said. In the old days, I used to hate being respectfully reminded that, being a woman,

I might not use the main entrance of the Athenaeum club. But even leaving this prejudice on one side, I do not find that the word 'respect' is adequate to the distinctions Williams himself has made in his discussion of our attitudes to the natural environment.

For in his essay Williams writes: 'Human beings have two basic kinds of emotional relations to nature: gratitude and a sense of peace on the one hand, terror and stimulation on the other'. And he notices an analogy between this psychological dichotomy and the late eighteenth-century philosophical and critical distinction between the beautiful and the sublime. He goes on: 'Not all our environmental concerns will be grounded in Promethean fear. Some of them will be grounded in our need for the other powers of nature, those associated with the beautiful'. I accept Williams's dichotomy, and his broad analogy between this distinction and that between the beautiful and the sublime. And it will be recalled that the concept of the sublime was closely associated by all those who examined it, not just with awe, but with actual fear, though of a partly hypothetical kind, since to experience aspects of nature as sublime, the human being who so experiences it must, it was often supposed, be in a position of actual safety. Poor Coleridge on his ledge of rock might seem a counterexample (see chapter 6, above). But, by his account, he rose above fear with the help of his Kantian reflections of human moral superiority.

I believe, however, that these two basic attitudes, which are both embedded in our value system, give rise to two different motives for seeking to preserve and not to destroy the natural environment. I do not think one can name our wish to safeguard that which is beautiful, whether in tamed or untamed nature, otherwise than by calling it love. Such love may of course be joined to 'respect', in Bernard Williams's sense of the word. Certainly Mr Page, the Cambridgeshire farmer, like any farmer must sometimes respect nature as a worthy and relentless enemy. But his lament for his loss of the old natural environment is the lament of a lover. It may be that sometimes that love will have to be sacrificed to economic necessity; and then the economists' questions will be asked: how much compensation will you demand? What price do you put on your sacrifice? And people will be offended by these questions, distinguishing between value and price. But they will always put up a fight against such sacrifices, and sometimes they will win, as they won the battle (at least for a time) to preserve the Forest of Dean.

I do not believe that such love of the natural world, intense though it may be, and central to the quality of life for many, can supply us with the motive we are looking for, to take responsibility for the planet as a whole. We accept responsibility for the things that we own and love; we may love and wish to conserve things that we do not own, but which in a looser sense we feel are ours. For these things we may also take responsibility, in that we will battle and campaign to keep them from harm. This is what Roger Scruton calls 'oikophilia', and upon which he asks us to confine ourselves. But it seems to me that we have a quite different motive for trying to accept and feel responsible for the global environment; and that motive is not love but fear: Promethean fear. The story of Prometheus was told in many forms, both in literature and in the visual arts, in sixth- and fifth-century BC Athens. Prometheus was chained to a rock to be tormented by Zeus in the form of an eagle, as a perpetual punishment for stealing fire, and thus introducing techne, skill, and so all civilisation, to mankind. The time of the greatest popularity of the myth coincided with a period of extraordinary advances in science, mathematics and technology in Greek-speaking Asia Minor and Athens. It is a myth that incorporates the lurking uneasiness that has always been felt about the encroachment of civilisation on nature.

If we turn our attention not to our parks and gardens, not even to ancient woodlands and other natural habitats, but to the environment as a whole, earth, water and air, we may, more and more, find ourselves asking: What have we done? What have we unleashed? What disaster will follow next? Nature can appear to be beyond our control after all. It is indifferent to our preferences and to our very existence. As it becomes apparent that it is our own technological ingenuity, our own greed and our own arrogance in assuming that we can do whatever suits us with the natural world which have brought about the environmental disasters we deplore, so our unease increases. In the UK and elsewhere in Europe we have always had occasional freak storms or long winters of snow and ice, exceptionally sunless and wet summers, destructive gales, floods and droughts. But these legendary occurrences, such as the frozen winter of 1947, or the rainless summer of 1976, were not seen by most people as capable of causal explanation, still less as the result of human activity. Now, however, not only do the floods, huge seas and gales seem more common, but we have learned to link them to our own technology. It is this new closeness to ourselves that makes us afraid.

And fear seems to me to be a powerful motive to bring us to adapt our behaviour and even to make sacrifices of some of the things that technology has brought us. If this means that we must educate people to be afraid, then we should reflect that this is, after all, a not uncommon purpose of education. We need think no further than education in public health: we have learned to fear tobacco, though this does not cause absolutely everyone to give up smoking; and we are slowly learning to fear sugar, though some of us retain our sweet tooth. And, as I have suggested, we have come quite a long way in our environmental education in the last fifty years. Let us resolve to persist in it; we have motive enough.

So that is the end of my critical reflections. I am conscious that there are aspects of ownership that I have not examined. But it is my hope that enough has come out of the questioning to show that it is a deeply rooted part of human nature to distinguish between what is mine and what is not. No other animals, though some may defend their nests or their wider territory, have the ability to institutionalise this possessive instinct, making laws to create and defend the rights of ownership. For human beings alone can not only envisage the past and the future as well as the present, the far off as well as the immediate, but can also articulate these visions in language, can think in general, as well as particular terms, and can create the concepts, central to ownership, of justice and rights. The power of language puts an immense distance between human animals and the rest of the animate and inanimate world. It is hardly to be wondered at that these same human beings have been arrogant enough to treat the rest of nature as if it were theirs, collectively, to use as they pleased. Perhaps, as others have suggested, it is time for a bit of humility, as well as fear, to regulate our dealings with our natural environment. Other animals can experience and display fear; no one who has ever ridden a nervous horse can doubt that. But no other animal can experience or display either arrogance or humility, for these are moral attributes, and none but we ourselves can practice morality.

Index